The Der
Papist R s
of 1705-6

Edited by Richard Clark

Derbyshire Record Society
Occasional Paper No. 5
1983

Published by the Derbyshire Record Society,
9 Caernarvon Close, Walton, Chesterfield, S40 3DY

First published 1983

ISBN 0 946324 02 6

Printed by D. J. Pryse & Son
Duffryn Road, Mountain Ash, Mid Glam.
Telephone (0443) 472791 & 472539

Contents

ABBREVIATIONS

A.A.B.	Archives of the Archbishop of Birmingham, Archbishop's House, Birmingham.
Bod. Lib.	Bodleian Library, Oxford.
D.A.J.	Journal of the Derbyshire Archaeological Society.
D.R.O.	Derbyshire Record Office.
H.L.R.O.	House of Lords Record Office.
H.M.C.	Historical Manuscripts Commission.
L.J.R.O.	Lichfield Joint Record Office.
P.R.O.	Public Record Office.

ACKNOWLEDGEMENTS

I first wish to acknowledge the kindness of the Clerk of the Records of the House of Lords and of Mr. M. B. S. Exham, Registrar of the diocese of Lichfield, who readily gave their permission for the publication of the Papist Returns. My thanks are also due to the staffs of the Derbyshire Record Office, the Lichfield Joint Record Office, the Bodleian Library and the Public Record Office and to Fr. F. Keegan, S.J. of Mount St. Mary's College, Spinkhill, and Fr. J. D. McEvilly, Keeper of the Archbishop of Birmingham's records. Finally I must thank the society's general editor, Mr. Philip Riden, for his ready assistance and sound advice.

Introduction

The Returns and their Origin

Two separate series of Papist Returns for the diocese of Coventry and Lichfield, of which the archdeaconry of Derby was a constituent part, have survived for the years 1705 and 1706.[1] The earlier set is among the archives of the House of Lords, the returns from the parishes having been bound in alphabetical order under their respective archdeaconries and these archdeaconries in the same order within each diocese.[2] The returns of 1706 are in the Lichfield Joint Record Office, in bundles in alphabetical order of parish.[3]

Both sets of returns originated from concern about the growth and prevalence of Popery as expressed in the House of Lords. On 2 March 1705 the Lords requested that the archbishops should direct their suffragans to 'take account of the number of Papists' in the parishes of their dioceses.[4] The Queen in Council subsequently ordered returns to be made. However, concern over Popery did not subside. On 28 February 1706 the gentry and clergy of Lancashire petitioned the House of Lords about the activities and growing numbers of Catholics in that county. As a result both the Commons and the Lords debated 'Prevention of Popery' bills, but, as Bishop Burnet explains, the idea of legislation was dropped because :

> So severe a law would be very unreasonable when we were in alliance with so many princes of that religion, and that it must lessen the force of the queen's intercession in favour of the Protestants that lived in the dominions of those princes.[5]

At this time the problem of maintaining foreign alliances in the war against France was more important than a domestic issue. Therefore the Lords sent an address to the Queen asking that a more careful watch be kept on Papists. On 4 April 1706 a Privy Council Order was made requiring the archbishops and their suffragans to make another survey of Catholics on similar lines to the returns of the previous year.[6]

The Catholic Threat and the Returns

Fear of Catholicism and of Catholics was deep-rooted in the political consciousness of most Englishmen of Queen Anne's reign. Its origins stemmed from the persecution of Protestants in the reign of Mary I (1553-58) and the attempts by Catholic conspirators, often backed by foreign Catholic powers, to overthrow Elizabeth, her successor, and Elizabeth's church settlement (1559). These events had been welded together with nationalist fervour by a skilful use of propaganda, often disguised as history, in which Catholicism and its adherents appeared as un-English, un-Christian and tyrannous, tools of foreign princes for enslaving a free people. This anti-Catholic mythology continued to develop during the seventeenth century, fuelled by the Gunpowder Plot of 1605, the activities of Catholics in the courts of Charles I and Charles II and the Popish Plot of 1678-9 at home, and the advance and aggressiveness of Catholic states in Europe during the Thirty Years War and the reign of Louis XIV. The succession of a Catholic king, James II, in 1685 proved a culmination and confirmation of many of the fears about Popery. His heavy-handed attempts to improve the lot of his co-religionists and to curb the privileges of the Established Church, together with the prominence of Catholics and their bishops at his court and in his government, united formerly opposed groups against him. When William of Orange invaded the country James's supporters rapidly dwindled and he fled to France.[7]

The Glorious Revolution of 1688 revived fears of Catholics because they now appeared politically more dangerous. James did not abandon his title and claims and set up a court at St. Germain under the protection of Louis XIV. Catholic Ireland rose in his support and this rebellion was crushed only with difficulty. Jacobite support in Scotland was strong among certain Highland clans and among the Episcopalians. There were numerous Jacobites in England and it was naturally feared that the English Catholics were loyal to, and desired, a Catholic king, especially as their vicars-apostolic upheld the rightful title of James and his male heir. The Catholics in England appeared now not only as fifth columnists secretly striving to fulfil the designs of the Pope, but also plotting the restoration of a deposed, unpopular and rejected king.

The political threat from Catholics did not ease with the death of James II in 1701 because Louis immediately recognised his son as James III of Great Britain and Ireland. The court of St. James still had a rival at St. Germain backed by the most powerful monarch in Europe. There were further succession problems. Queen Anne was prematurely old, unhealthy and, after 1700, childless. In 1703 the Scots Parliament declared its own right to choose a successor to the Scots throne, making it clear that Scotland was not bound to accept the English Act of Settlement of 1701 to ensure a Protestant succession. The spectre of the Pretender invading the realm with French aid and of civil war after Anne's death haunted politicians. Against this background the returns of 1705 and 1706 were made to inform the authorities of potential troublemakers.

The Organization and Content of the Enquiries made for the Returns

The returns of 1705 and 1706 were organised in almost the same way. The archbishop of Canterbury wrote to the bishop of Coventry and Lichfield, who in turn required the incumbents and churchwardens of each parish in 1705 and the incumbents only in 1706 to draw up returns and bring them to the bishop's probate courts. Returns from parishes in the northern deaneries of High Peak and Chesterfield were to be sent to the court at Chesterfield; those from the parishes in the southern deaneries of Castillar, Ashbourne, Derby and Repton were to be taken to the court in All Saints, Derby. After being collected at the courts the 1705 returns were sent up to Westminster, but the 1706 returns got no further than the diocesan registry.

In 1705 incumbents had only to list the names of Papists or reputed Papists in their respective parishes. The enquiries for the 1706 returns were more searching. The Privy Council Order to the Archbishop required:

> The clergy . . . to take an exact and particular account of the number of Papists and reputed Papists in every parish with their qualities, estates and places of abode and to return the same to their respective diocesans . . . And it is Her Majesty's further pleasure that Your Grace do require the several bishops within your Province by all proper ways and means to inform themselves what advowsons or rights of presentation or donation of churches, benefices or schools are in the hands of any Papists or reputed Papists or of any in trust for them and to return what they shall find.[8]

The bishop in turn required his clergy to inform him of patronage held by Catholics in their returns. As a result of the references to schools or of the lack of them the returns of 1706 are more interesting than those of 1705.

The Results of the Enquiries

Both in 1705 and 1706 the bishop failed to receive returns from all the parishes within the Archdeaconry of Derby. At the beginning of the bound 1705 returns there is a contemporary note saying that for Ashford, Buxton, Hartington, Long Eaton, Sheldon and Earl's Sterndale: 'There are not any returns come in, altho' the ministers thereof have been several times required to send in the same'. In addition returns are lacking for Eyam and the chapelries of Alsop en le Dale, Ballidon, Derwent, Breaston and Risley, although in the cases of the chapelries they may have been included in the returns from their mother churches. The chief difficulty appears to have been obtaining returns from peculiars outside archdiaconal jurisdiction. All the parishes in the note of missing returns were in peculiars.

Even within the episcopal jurisdiction the authorities were not entirely successful in procuring returns on time. By the time the bishop's probate court sat at Chesterfield on 26 June 1705 it is clear that the incumbents and churchwardens of the northern deaneries had not had time to complete returns. Out of the 49 dated returns from these deaneries only 23 were dated on or before 26 June. The returns from 23 parishes were not made until November 1705. The two days extra grace given to the incumbents of the southern deaneries resulted in a larger proportion of returns from these deaneries being sent to the court at Derby in time for its sitting on 28 June. However, at least seventeen returns were not made until November, and the return from Elvaston was not made until 8 December 1705.

It was probably on account of the difficulties encountered in procuring returns during 1705 that the Privy Council urged the archbishop to take disciplinary action against the clergy who failed to make returns in 1706 :

> And your Grace is likewise to require such bishops in their respective dioceses to proceed against such of the clergy as shall refuse or neglect to do their duty in respect to the said service according to the utmost severity of the law and also to return the names of the clergy who shall be defective in performing the said service.[8]

Nevertheless some incumbents did not make returns. There is a contemporary list of defaulting parishes among the returns, consisting of Bolsover, Fenny Bentley, Hathersage, Horsley, Kirk Langley, Wirksworth, Longstone (but a return for Longstone exists), Breaston, Calke, Dale Abbey, Hartington and Earl Sterndale. In addition returns are lacking for the parish of St. Michael's, Derby, and the chapelries of Alsop en le Dale, Hognaston, Twyford, Ashford, Brassington, Ballidon, Brimington, Belper, Heage, Turnditch, Boulton, Fairfield, Denby, Smalley, Bretby, Risley and Rosliston. Again it is possible that some of the chapelries were included in the returns for the mother churches, or that some returns have been lost since 1706. However, the authorities were more successful in procuring the returns of 1706 on time. All but two had been sent in by the end of 1706. The last to be received was from Youlgreave, dated 14 April 1707.

A comparison of the two sets of returns reveals startling differences. Identical returns were made from only eight of the fifty-three parishes from which Papists were returned both years. Before condemning the returns as grossly inaccurate and unreliable at least two factors have to be borne in mind. First, the incumbents, required to provide the names of Papists, were given no guide-lines on how to go about the task. The result was that Papists were returned in a variety of ways. Some incumbents listed whole families, others husbands and wives only and others heads of households only. There were ministers who changed their methods of listing from the one year to the next. The rector of Brailsford returned the whole of the Aston family in 1705 and only its head in 1706. In the early eighteenth century there was little notion of the modern methods of taking a census, i.e. counting every living member of the community. The first official census of the whole population was not taken until 1801. In 1705 and 1706 there were a variety of precedents for guidance. Lists for taxation purposes often named householders and freeholders. Previous attempts at calculating religious allegiance were made in 1603, when the numbers of communicants and recusants in each diocese were listed, and in 1676 (the Compton Census) when everyone of sixteen years of age or over was enumerated under the heading of Conformist, Dissenter or Papist. The Recusancy Laws, designed to curb Catholics, also suggested different ways of returning Papists. By a statute of 1606 everyone over nine years of age failing to attend Anglican services on four consecutive Sundays was liable to be convicted as a recusant. Parish constables and churchwardens were supposed to present lists of such offenders to the Quarter Sessions at least once a year. By the same statute recusants convicted could suffer the confiscation of two-thirds of their real estate and the whole of their personal goods and chattels. However, minors, wives (as **femmes covertes** under Common Law) and the propertyless were unaffected by these threats and thus excluded from the attentions of Exchequer Recusancy Commissions. Therefore careful account has to be made of the different ways incumbents returned Papists and their families when comparing the two sets of returns.

The second factor is that between the making of the two returns Papists actually appeared in or disappeared from certain parishes. In one case the burial of a Papist, named in 1705 but dead by the time of the 1706 return, has been traced.[9] Some Papists recorded in one year only were members of the more mobile sections of early eighteenth-century society, for example; Michael Sherwood, a day-labourer who had moved from Tideswell to Edensor; William Thompson, footboy to the Countess of Bellamont; Edward Nettleton 'who is sometimes a journeyman to a hatter', but who presumably found work elsewhere when not so employed.[10]

Despite these explanations it is still clear that some of the differences between the returns stemmed from the carelessness and incompetence of those who made them. A good example occurs from Weston upon Trent. In 1705 the churchwardens informed the bishop that there were no Papists living in the parish. A year later the incumbent returned ten members of the Brown family. The parish register makes it clear that the Browns were not new to the parish and that their religious affiliations were already well-known, for towards the end of the register there is a page specially devoted to the baptisms of Papists' children. On this page the baptisms of the Brown children are recorded in 1698, 1699, 1701, 1703 and 1705 (twins).[11]

Similar examples can be multiplied, and stimulate some uneasy questions. Do the returns record accurately the Catholics and Catholic communities living in Derbyshire in 1705 and 1706? Is one set of returns more accurate than the other? Is there any hope of procuring useful statistics from the seemingly conflicting evidence?

One problem in answering the first question is the lack of contemporary comparative material. The constables' presentments of Papists in the Quarter Sessions papers are scanty by the early 1700s,[12] and the records stemming from the Registration of Papists' Estates Acts of 1714 and 1717 refer to propertied Catholics only. The only solution is to investigate earlier records of Catholics in pre-1700 constables' presentments, the Recusants Rolls (1591-1689), Visitation comperta (in which large numbers of popish recusants appear from 1609 to 1693 and smaller numbers until 1702) and the Compton Census of 1676 in order to ascertain the parishes in which Catholicism was traditionally strong and to see whether the incumbents of these parishes returned Papists in 1705-6 or not.[13] Such an investigation shows that large numbers of Papists were returned in 1705-6 from communities in which Catholics had long been numerous, for example, Hathersage, Eckington, Norbury and Tideswell. There is no evidence that any substantial Catholic community was overlooked. Since 1676 Catholics had disappeared from certain parishes, particularly in the south-west of Derbyshire — Barton Blount, Doveridge, Edlaston, Etwall, Somersall Herbert and Sutton on the Hill, but these cases can be explained by the removal, apostasy or extinction of prominent Catholic families, such as the Gerards, the Merrys and the Fitzherberts of Somersall Herbert, before and after the Compton Census. Catholics were seldom, if ever, recorded in these parishes during the eighteenth century. Catholic communities were identified in 1705 and 1706, even if the numbers of Catholics within them were not accurately assessed.[14]

From this conclusion one is able to proceed a step further in answering the question whether useful statistics can be reaped from the returns or not. Both sets name a similar number of individuals — 225 in 1705 and 239 in 1706. If the individuals in both sets of returns are collated a grand total of 316 Papists and reputed Papists is obtained. Of this total 148 names are common to both returns. The other 161 can be accounted for as follows :

27 from 4 parishes which made a return in 1705 but not in 1706.

6 from Eyam which has a return for 1706 but not for 1705.

11 close relatives (husband, wife, brother, sister, mother, child) named in 1705 but not in 1706, but whose families, or at least one member thereof, were common to both returns.

14 close relatives as above but mentioned in 1706 and not in 1705.

39 other individuals mentioned only in 1705.

71 other individuals mentioned only in 1706.

Even after the figures have been adjusted for missing returns and for close relatives (to account for some of the vagaries in the methods of returning Papists) over a third of the grand total of Papists is unaccounted for. However, the results show that the 1706 returns, despite defects, were more informative than those of the previous year, but such are the defects in both sets of returns that it is only by collating them that there is any hope of obtaining information approaching completeness.

In comparison with earlier and later attempts to enumerate Catholics in Derbyshire the grand total of 316 appears small. 596 Papists were listed in the Compton Census of 1676 and 748 Papists in the Returns of 1767.[15] However, in the former case Papists sixteen years of age and over were included and in the latter whole Papist families were returned. In 1705-6 few wives and fewer children were listed, and so the figures are not directly comparable. To obtain an estimate of the number of Catholics in 1705-6 the males (excluding sons) in the returns have been counted. As the majority of these can be assumed to have been heads of households a multiplier of 4.25 has been applied, resulting in a total of 811. To acquire an estimate of Catholics in 1676 a multiplier of 1.5 has been used to account for children excluded from the census, giving a total of 894. Dr. Bossy's investigations have led him to conclude that the 1767 returns under-estimated the Catholic population by around 15 per cent.[16] If such an adjustment is made a total of 860 is obtained. The total for 1705-6 is somewhat high in that no account has been made for the mobile elements of the Catholic population which were less likely to have been heads of households. Although the results of these calcul- ations are in relative agreement, overall those for 1705-6 are probably on the low side. In the notes the returns of Hathersage and Bakewell are indicated as under-estimates, and these, perhaps with a few others, probably account for the deficiency. In any case it is clear that Catholic numbers were virtually static for a century, despite government fears to the contrary.

The returns, specially those of 1706, also refer to the landed wealth of the richer Papists. Again the details in the two sets of returns do not always agree. For example, William Fitzherbert's estates in Norbury were valued at £400 p.a. in 1705 and £618 p.a. in 1706. The valuations in the returns can also be compared with those given by the Papists themselves after they were required to register their estates by the Acts of 1714 and 1717. In some cases there are considerable differences between the assessments of the clergy and those of the Papists. The clergy were nearly always too conservative in their estimates. Robert Beaumont's lands in 1705-6 were valued at £40 p.a., but he assessed them at £89 14s p.a. The Hunloke estates were valued at £1,000 p.a. in 1705-6 and £1,800 p.a. in 1717.[17] The cause of these differences was often that the clergy only had sufficient knowledge to assess the estates which lay in their own parishes or nearby. However, the estates of some Papists were widespread. Thus the curate of Wingerworth appears to have paid no account of the Hunloke estates further south in the county at West Hallam, Mapperley and Kirk Hallam. Nor do the returns provide a complete list of Papists' estates in Derbyshire. A number of

Papists registered in Derbyshire but were not mentioned in the returns because they did not live in the county. Among the most notable were the Willoughbys of Cossall, Nottinghamshire, who had estates in Wilne and Kirk Hallam; the Duke of Norfolk, who had a small estate at Whitwell; and Lord Clifford, who owned the lease of the lot and cope of lead in the King's Field, Wirksworth.[18] These Catholics were excluded because the enquiries of 1706 only required that the estates of the Papists living in the parish in question should be mentioned, and the clergy were unwilling to go beyond their commission. Therefore the value of estates in the returns should only be taken as approximate valuations of the lands in or near the parish in which the Papists mentioned normally resided or possessed a residence.

The returns also fail to provide a complete list of patronage in Catholic hands. According to them Papists owned the advowsons of Norbury with Snelston and Glossop, the third turn of presentation to Shirland and a governorship of Repton School. The incumbents of Barrow upon Trent and West Hallam claimed the advowsons of their livings were not held by Papists, but, in reality, they were owned by the Catholic Beaumont and Hunloke families respectively.[19] In both these livings the Papist owners had previously granted or sold the next turns of presentation to conformists in order to prevent the University of Cambridge acquiring the presentations during their recusancy, which would otherwise have happened under Acts passed in 1605-6 and 1689. It is probable that the two incumbents did not mention the Catholic owners of the advowsons because the instructions in the Privy Council Order did not take into account grants of turns of presentation by Catholics to others, but asked simply 'what advowsons or rights of presentation . . . are in the hands of any Papist.' The presentations to Barrow and West Hallam at that present time technically were not in the hands of Papists. Anthony Trollope, rector of Norbury, was less devious in his interpretation of the instructions and his return clearly shows the Fitzherberts allowing conformists to present in their stead. Even with the addition of the livings of Barrow and West Hallam, however, the returns show that Catholics held very little patronage in Derbyshire. In the county there were over one hundred benefices, but Papists possessed the advowsons of only four of them in full.

The returns of 1705-6 are incomplete and the information within them at first glance appears inaccurate, careless or conflicting. However, by collating the two sets, analysing the methods by which Papists were returned and making allowance for some of the limitations of the returns, useful information can be drawn from them. Despite the difficulties they present they are still an important source for the history of early eighteenth-century English Catholicism.

The Catholic Community in 1705-6

The returns give two immediate impressions : first that the Catholics in Derbyshire were an overwhelmingly rural group, and second that most Catholics were concentrated in a few communities — Ashbourne, Barlborough, Dronfield, Eckington, Hathersage, Norbury, Tideswell, West Hallam and Wingerworth — and were not at all widespread. In most Derbyshire parishes there were no Papists.

In Chesterfield and Derby, the two boroughs in the county, there were only three Papists. The only market town which could claim a substantial Catholic community living in the town itself, and not in surrounding hamlets, was Ashbourne. The urbanisation of English Catholicism was a later development. As a consequence the returns name very few Papists whose occupations in the professions or in wholesale or retail trade were characteristically urban. Otherwise the Papists in the returns came from a wide spectrum of society. There were members of the gentry, including Sir Henry Hunloke 'knight and baronet'; prosperous tenant farmers like Charles Aston of Brailsford; yeomen and husbandmen; men plying traditional crafts such as Francis Greensmith of Ashbourne, a tailor, John Hall of Cubley, shoemaker, and Ignatius Woomack of Dronfield, glover; others employed in newer or more capitalised rural industries such as the stockingers in Ilkeston and West Hallam and the colliers in Staveley; day labourers; and paupers dependent on alms like William Cooper of Snelston and his wife. The Catholics were represented in nearly all the strata of early eighteenth-century society. They were exceptional in their religion rather than their social status and occupations. The social structure of Catholicism contrasted with that of contemporary Protestant Dissent, which drew its members chiefly from the middle bands of society and seldom attracted support from the very rich or the very poor. Also unlike Catholicism, Protestant Dissent flourished in the towns.[20]

Although Catholics came from many walks of life they were confined to a few communities. Most of these communities had one common factor: a member of the Catholic gentry living within them or possessing large estates in the neighbourhood. Such people often maintained a priest and a mission. This was true in the case of Ashbourne (the Pegges and Whitehalls), Hassop in Bakewell parish (the Eyres), Barlborough (the Poles), Eckington (the Poles), Norbury (the Fitzherberts), West Hallam (the Hunlokes) and Wingerworth (the Hunlokes).[21]

In the surrounding parishes where the Catholic gentry also had estates there were smaller satellite communities of Catholics, for example in Snelston near Norbury and Staveley near Eckington. Only in Tideswell, Wormhill and Hathersage, remote in the High Peak, were there large numbers of Catholics without a dominant Catholic gentry family. Even in these places Catholicism had been stimulated, nurtured and preserved by the activities of wealthy, influential men in the later sixteenth and early seventeenth centuries.[22] The Derbyshire Catholics were not exceptional. Catholics elsewhere tended to cluster around dominant Catholic families. In Wiltshire the Catholics by 1706 were mostly concentrated on the estates of Lord Arundell of Wardour, Lord Stourton of Stourton, the Webbs of Odstock and the Mores of Wootton Bassett.[23] Once such influential people apostasised, died without heirs or moved away, Catholics seldom survived for long in their old strongholds, as in the case of the Merrys, Fitzherberts of Somersall Herbert and the Gerards in south-west Derbyshire.

The reasons why Catholics should cluster around Catholic gentry are not hard to imagine. The gentry had social and economic influence which could be extended not only over their households and servants but also their tenants. In the Wingerworth return of 1705 two of Sir Henry Hunloke's servants are mentioned. Samuel Greensmith and Widow Brown were listed as tenants on the Hunloke estate in 1717.[24] But it must not be thought that the Papists of 1705-6 were Catholics solely on account of crude pressures inflicted upon them by their social superiors. The Hunlokes had many more tenants on their Wingerworth estate who presumably were conformists in 1706. Even in the largest Catholic communities in Derbyshire the incumbents do not suggest that the Catholics were other than a sizeable minority of their parishioners. The importance of the Catholic gentry was their ability to provide facilities and security for worship, the means to support missionary priests and a social presence under which lesser mortals with similar inclinations in religion could shelter away from a hostile world.[25]

Earlier the fear with which Catholicism was regarded was described, but the Catholics in the returns do not appear particularly fearsome. On the contrary they seem quiet, unremarkable members of the public. The vicar of Ilkeston noted that the Papists of that parish were 'not being of an unquiet or uncivil disposition or carriage'. Only John Easom of Ashbourne's behaviour appears to have given offence. Conflicts over religious matters, such as recent conversions, matters of doctrine or over the rites of passage, are not mentioned in the returns. The curate of Kniveton refers to William Tipper's 'perversion' by a Papist family with distaste but not animosity, and he also notes that Tipper's wife was a 'Protestant of the Church of England'. Obviously the Tippers did not find their religious differences insurmountable. The parochial incumbents also made little effort to report Catholic priests and their missions. Robert Percy, the missioner at Spinkhill, was the only priest mentioned. The priests at Yeldersley, Hassop, Hathersage and Wingerworth were ignored. In 1705-6 the Derbyshire Catholics appear to have been well-intergrated into their local communities and were the source of little disturbance. Even Anglican clergymen had learned to live with them (and their priests) in relative harmony.

Such was the gap between the threatening theory behind the anti-Catholic mythology and the reality that the Catholics, barely one per cent of the population, lacked the influence and numbers to pose a serious political problem, that little action was taken by Parliament after the returns were made. The only legislation against Catholics in Queen Anne's reign was an Act of 1713 effectively removing ecclesiastical patronage from their hands.

Methods of Transcription

Only the returns which give some solid information (i.e. reference to Papists, patrons, schools or lack of schools) have been transcribed. In other cases the existence of a return had been noted by the phrase 'Nil Return'. To avoid repetition introductory phrases such as 'To the Right Reverend Father in God John by divine providence Lord Bishop of Coventry and Lichfield' and geographical expressions such as 'in the county of Derby and diocese of Coventry and Lichfield' have been omitted, and the omissions indicated by three dots. Otherwise the returns have been fully transcribed. Spelling has been modernised, except of surnames, and punctation has been amended for the sake of clarity. Contractions and abbreviations have been transcribed at length. There has been no revision of the grammar and syntax of the returns. Dates are New Style. An asterisk (★) at the head of an entry indicates that the parish is included in the 'Notes to the Returns' on pp. 29 - 36.

References

1. The archdeaconry of Derby was virtually co-terminous with the ancient bounds of the county. No account has been taken of modern boundary changes in this work.
2. H.L.R.O., Papist Returns 1705-6.
3. L.J.R.O., Papist Returns B/A. 12i.
4. H.M.C., **House of Lords MSS 1704-6** (1912) vi, 416.
5. G. Burnet, **History of my own Time** (Oxford, 1823) v, 200.
6. Some of the 1706 returns were written on the backs of the printed orders.
7. J. C. H. Aveling, **The Handle and the Axe : the Catholic Recusants in England from Reformation to Emancipation** (London, 1976); J. Bossy, **The English Catholic Community 1570-1850** (London, 1975); R. Clifton, 'Fear of Popery' in C. Russell (ed.), **The Origins of the English Civil War** (London, 1973); J. P. Kenyon, **The Popish Plot** (London, 1972); J. Miller, **Popery and Politics in England 1660-1688** (Cambridge, 1973).
8. L.J.R.O., Papist Returns 1706 B/A/12i for copies of the order.
9. See the returns and the note for Stanley.
10. See the returns for Edensor, Swarkeston and Whittington.
11. D.R.O., Weston-upon-Trent Parish Register 1610-1740, D1408/PI1.
12. D.R.O., Quarter Sessions Papers 1702, 1704, 1707, 1714.

13. D.R.O., Quarter Sessions Papers, 1634, 1639, 1683, 1684, 1689, 1690, 1693-6, 1698-9; P.R.O., Recusant Rolls E377/1-82; L.J.R.O., Visitation Comperta B/V/1/26, 30, 41, 44, 59, 64, 72, 79; Citations B/V/4, 1677, 1693, 1698, 1702; J. C. Cox, **Three Centuries of Derbyshire Annals** (London, 1890), i, 292-5.

14. For further details see: R. Clark, 'Anglicanism, Recusancy and Dissent in Derbyshire 1603-1730' (Unpublished Oxford D.Phil Thesis, 1979), 184-7.

15. Cox, op. cit., 292-5 (His total of 588 is erroneous. The correct entry for Dronfield is 517 Conformists, 4 Papists and 9 Dissenters); H.L.R.O., Papist Return Abstracts, 1767.

16. J. Bossy, **The English Catholic Community 1578-1850** (London, 1975), 184.

17. See under Wingerworth; P.R.O., Forfeited Estates Papers FEC1/1139.

18. P.R.O., Forfeited Estates Papers FEC1/1139.

19. See notes under these parishes.

20. M. R. Watts, **The Dissenters from the Reformation to the French Revolution** (Oxford, 1978), 352-5.

21. See notes under these parishes.

22. See notes under these parishes.

23. J. A. Williams, 'Wiltshire Catholics in the Early Eighteenth Century: the diocesan returns of 1706', **Recusant History,** vii (1963), 11-22.

24. P.R.O., Forfeited Estates Papers FEC1/1139.

25. Clark, Thesis, 37-69, 183-194.

The Returns

1. ALFRETON

7 Nov. 1705: Nil Return. Samuel Dudson, vicar.

30 Sept. 1706: This may testify whom it may concern that there is neither Papist nor reputed Papist that I know of in the parish of Alfreton. Neither is the presentation of that church in the disposition of any Papist or reputed Papist. Neither have we any free school founded in our parish by Papist, reputed Papist or any other. Samuel Dudson, vicar.

2. ALLESTREE AND QUARNDON

12 Nov. 1705: Nil Return. Jasper Horsington, minister; Jacob Wall and William Baily, churchwardens.

1706: See 99.

3. ALVASTON

1705: See 117.

4 Oct. 1706: Nil Return. Hugh Broom, curate.

4. ASHBOURNE AND MAPLETON*

1705: The names of all such persons within the parishes of Ashbourne and Mapleton as are Papists or may be justly so reputed: Mr. Charles Pegg, gent., his wife and family; George Pegg, husbandman, and his family; Mr. Whitehall has an estate here but resides at London; Gilbert Swift, hardware-seller, his wife and son; Robert Sheldon, barber, and his wife; Francis Greensmith, tailor, and his wife; John Ditch, labourer; John Easom, carpenter and fornicator at this time under commutation with the Court at Lichfield, who hopes that on payment of his last portion of his commutation money the court will please to dismiss his poor fellow sinner, Elizabeth Hampson, against whom excommunication is issued, only because she is poor and unable to compound, but he hopes so large a sum as he pays may compensate for both or else (he says) he could have compounded cheaper in his own Church of Rome. This is a true copy of the writing under the hand of Mr. Nathaniel Boothouse, directed to me by way of letter without any names subscribed unto it, carefully examined by me. Richard Raine, N.S.

1706: In obedience to your Lordship's commands and in pursuance of the order of Her Majesty's most honourable Privy Council therewith sent me I have used the best endeavour I can to give a full and satisfactory account of the names, qualities and estates of all Papists or reputed Papists within my parish. But my parish (in the out hamlets of it) is so large, and the time since my settlement in it so short, that it is impossible I should yet know every family within it or be able to give any exact account of the value of their several estates. Upon the best enquiry I can make, I hope this following account will prove satisfactory, which, I believe, is exact enough in the names and number of Papists or justly so reputed within the parish of Ashbourne in the County of Derby, viz: Mr. Gilbert Whitehall, goldsmith or banker in London and there usually resident, has an estate in Yeldersley within the said parish of £200 per annum as some persons value it, though others say it is not as much. Mr. Charles Pegge, a wife and daughter, has an estate in Yeldersley aforesaid of about £100 per annum, though others value it but at £80 per annum or under. George Pegge of Yeldersley aforesaid, farmer or husbandman and his family. In Ashbourne town are these: Gilbert Swift, seller of hardware, his wife and son; Robert Sheldon, barber and his wife; Francis Greensmith, tailor, and his wife; John Ditch, weaver; John Easom, carpenter —— Woodward, a poor journeyman or labourer. There is no advowson or presentation to church or school belonging to any of these that I know of. The advowson of Ashbourne cum Mapleton belongs to the Dean of Lincoln, and the great tithes and chief of the small tithes (that is to say wool and lamb) throughout the whole parish are enjoyed or taken by the dean's lessee and his under-tenants, and nothing is left to the poor vicar but his Easter Roll, not really worth £15 per annum. He wishes that he . . . get an augmentation or knew how to recommend his vicarage to Her Majesty's Bounty. In the small village of Mapleton near Ashbourne are no Papists nor reputed Papists. Nathaniel Boothouse, vicar.

5. ASHOVER

29 June 1705: Nil Return. Obadiah Bourne, rector; Edward Ragg, churchwarden.

24 Sept. 1706: Nil Return. Obadiah Bourne, rector.

6. ASTON-UPON-TRENT

28 June 1705: Nil Return. Robert Bingham and Christopher Fairebrother, churchwardens.

4 Oct. 1706: Nil Return. Thomas Holden, rector.

7. ATLOW

28 June 1705: Nil Return. Ralph Burton, curate.

3 Oct. 1706: There is neither Papist nor reputed Papist dwelling within the liberty or chapelry of Atlow in the parish of Bradbourne . . . And as for the donation of our chapel it is not in the disposition of any Papist or reputed Papist nor in any other in trust for any such person. We have no school etc. Ralph Burton, curate.

8. AULT HUCKNALL

26 June 1705: Nil Return. Roger Lowde, vicar; Richard Jackson and Thomas Saunders, churchwardens.

2 Sept. 1706: I, the vicar of the parish aforesaid, whose name is subscribed, do certify that there is no Papist or reputed Papist in our parish save only William Hall, a journeyman to a clock-maker; and likewise I further certify that the right of presentation or donation of our church or school is not in the disposition of any Papist or reputed Papist, or any other in trust for any such person. Roger Lowde, vicar.

9. BAKEWELL

1705: The parish of Bakewell in the Peak, although it be very large, having nine chapels in it besides the mother church, yet hath very few Papists in it and those very inconsiderable. The only person of note is Rowland Eyre, esquire, dwelling sometime in Hassop. There is one Charles Baker dwelling in the same town. I cannot find out anymore but what the Curate of Baslow hath returned. Thomas Wilson, vicar.

8 Oct. 1706: In the body of the church of Bakewell, that is the chapels being excluded, there is not any one Papist or reputed Papist, save only in the hamlet of Hassop where at present resideth Thomas Eyre, squire, and several of his servants, both men and maids, whose names I know not; nor hath the said Mr. Eyre any advowsons or donations of any church or chapel or school in the whole High Peak, and his estate there is commonly reputed about two hundred pounds a year. This is all I can testify under my hand. Thomas Wilson, vicar.

10. BARLBOROUGH*

25 June 1705: The number, quality and estates of the Papists or reputed Papists in the parish of Barlborough: 1. Mr. Boden, a widower and person of some small estate. 2. Richard Willoughby, a labouring man. 3. Robert Savage, a labourer in the coal mines. 4. John Johnson, a musician. 5. George Corker, a labouring man. 6. George Lenthall, a gardener. 8. George Gee, a labouring man. 9. Nicholas Lenthall, a labouring man or gardener. 10. Robert Pattison, a shoemaker. 11. Michael Siddal, labourer. James Cook, rector.
(There is no seventh name).

2 Oct. 1706: In the parish of Barlborough there are such Papists as are named in the following account 2 Oct. 1706: Mr. Boden of Beighton Fields, yeoman, his estate about £16 per annum; Richard Willoughby, labourer; Michael Siddal; George and Thomas Corker, sons of Widow Corker, labourers; John Johnson, fidler; George Gee, labourer; Thomas Lenthall, shopkeeper; Robert Pattison, shoemaker. The advowson or right of presentation or donation of our church is not in the disposition of any Papist or reputed Papist or of any other in trust for any such person. There is no school founded or in the disposition of any Papist or reputed Papist in our parish. James Cook, rector.

11. BARLOW

9 Nov. 1705: Nil Return. Edward Calton, curate.

2 Oct. 1706: Nil Return. Edward Calton, curate.

12. BARROW UPON TRENT*

28 June 1706: We have living in our parish Robert Beaumont, gentleman, a Papist who may have an estate of about £40 per annum, and his wife, who are both Papists. These are all the Papists or reputed Papists within our parish. Robert Norman, vicar; John Alt and William Ensor, churchwardens.

1706: These are to certify whom it may concern that there is neither Papist nor reputed Papist in the parish of Barrow super Trent in the County of Derby save one Mr. Beaumont who has an estate in the said parish of about £40 per annum, and that the presentation of the church of Barrow aforesaid is not in any Papist or reputed Papist or in any other person in trust for any Papist or reputed Papist. And likewise there is no school in the said parish. Robert Norman, vicar.

13. BARTON BLOUNT*

22 Nov. 1705: Mr. Fisher: I received yours [letter] and am sorry that I had not seen it sooner because I was with Mr. Chancellor the 13th instant but heard no word of this affair. As to Barton Blount the people have no public place for the worship and service of God, the church being destroyed in the English Wars and never yet rebuilt, for which reason Mr. John Allsopp, the minister, lives remote, and the parishioenrs go to what church they please, some to Boyleston, some to Church Broughton, some to Sutton and, as I hear, some to the meetings. Amongst those that come to Boyleston is Mr. Simpson who is the chief man in the parish: he was educated some years at St. John's College, Cambridge. I have often seen him at church, when he stayed the whole time of divine service and sermon. Give my humble service to Mr. Chancellor. Thomas Allsopp.

1 Oct. 1706: Nil Return. John Allsopp, minister.

14. BASLOW

1705: A true account of all the Papists within our chapelry of Baslow: Ralph Frost of Calver, wire drawer, and Sarah, his wife, and two sons. Joseph Nicholls, curate.

7 Oct. 1706: An exact and particular account of the number of Papists or reputed Papists within our chapelry of Baslow in the parish of Bakewell and county of Derby with their quality, estates and places of abode as followeth: Ralph Frost of Calver, a poor wire drawer, and Sarah, his wife, and three sons: one is an apprentice to a stocking weaver, and one daughter-in-law Anne Ragge. Joseph Nichols, curate.

15. BEELEY

13 Nov. 1705: Nil Return. Gavin Ferne, curate.

7 Oct. 1706: These may certify whom it may concern that we have neither Papist nor reputed Papist dwelling within our parochial chapelry of Beeley, and that the right of presentation or donation of our chapel is in the disposition of the Dean of Lichfield, and that there is no school founded in the abovesaid chapelry. Gavin Ferne, curate; Samuel Grundy, chapelwarden.

16. BEIGHTON

26 June 1705: Nil Return. Robert Shirte, Thomas Hurte, churchwardens.

1 Oct. 1706: This is to certify whom it may concern that, after the strictest enquiry, I can hear no Papists or reputed Papists dwelling in the parish of Beighton, nor of any estates, presentations or any other endowments belonging to any such persons. There is one school founded in the parish. Marmaduke Drake, vicar.

17. BELPER

1705: Nil Return. Joseph Gorwey, vicar of Duffield.

1706: No Return.

18. BLACKWELL

26 June 1705: Nil Return. Samuel Strutt, churchwarden; Sampson Rogers, vicar.

1706: Nil Return. Sampson Rogers, curate.

19. BOLSOVER

1705: There is only one woman a Papist or reputed Papist, named Mary Stancer, the wife of John Stancer, in the parish of Bolsover, a tobacco pipe-maker, which is all of any degree or quality whatsoever. Richard Chadwick, vicar; Robert Machan, Robert White, churchwardens.

1706: No Return.

20. BONSALL

28 June 1705: Nil Return. John Eaton and Abram Woodneis, churchwardens.

13 Dec. 1706: In pursuance of a letter from his Lordship the Bishop of Lichfield and Coventry by the commands of His Grace the Archbishop of Canterbury these are to certify that there is no Papists or reputed Papists dwelling within the parish of Bonsall in the county of Derby and that the presentation to the said church of Bonsall doth belong to the Dean of Lincoln for the time being, and that there is not any school founded at present within the said parish. Godard Knighton, rector.

21. BOYLESTON

28 June 1705: Nil Return. Thomas Alsopp, rector.

1 Oct. 1706: Nil Return. Thomas Allsopp, rector.

22. BRADBOURNE

28 June 1705: Nil Return. Robert Gettliff, vicar; Thomas Wills and Robert Bomford, churchwardens.

1 Oct. 1706: Having received the commands of my Lord the Bishop of Lichfield and Coventry to take an exact and particular account of the number of Papists and reputed Papists dwelling within my parish of Bradbourne in the county of Derby with their qualities and estates, and to give account thereof at the next probate court held in Derby, and also to inform my lord bishop whether the advowson or right of presentation of my church or of any school founded within my parish be in the disposition of any Papists or reputed Papists or of any other in trust for any such person, this is to certify whom it may concern that according to the best of my knowledge and enquiry there is no single person a Papist or reputed Papist within the precincts of my parish (except one ordinary man living within the chapelry of Tissington, a member of my parish, an account of which I refer and leave to the curate there to give in at the probate court). Neither is the right of presentation of my church . . . nor any school founded within my parish in the disposition of any Papist or reputed Papist or in any other in trust for any such person. Robert Getliffe.

23. BRADLEY

28 June 1705: Nil Return. William Hawford, rector.

2 Oct. 1706: I, William Hawford, rector of Bradley in the county of Derby do hereby certify that there are no Papists or reputed Papists within the parish of Bradley aforesaid. And I do also further certify that the advowson . . . is in the disposition of the Reverend the Dean of Lincoln. Do hereby certify that we have no school in our parish.

24. BRAILSFORD

27 June 1705: There is in our parish but one man that professes the Romish religion, whose name is Charles Aston and who is the tenant of a farm of about £26 per annum belonging to the lord of the manor, having with him his wife, daughter and sister, which three persons are also Papists. Samuel Labonneille, rector; George Boam and William Withnold, churchwardens.

25. BRAILSFORD AND OSMASTON BY ASHBOURNE

4 Oct. 1706: I, whose name is here subscribed, do certify to your lordship that there is no Papist or reputed Papist in the said parish of Brailsford but one, whose name is Charles Aston, who renteth an estate of £22 per annum belonging to the Right Honourable the Lord Ferrers, who is lord of the manor and patron of the living or rectory of the said parish, to which I was presented by his lordship. I also certify to your lordship that in the parish of Osmaston-upon-Ashbourne in the said county of Derby, belonging to the rectory of Brailsford, there is no Papist but one, named Thomas Holdaker, who renteth in it an estate of about £30 a year belonging to one named George Pegge, a farmer, who liveth now in the parish of West Hallam and is a Papist. I do also certify to your lordship that there is no public founded school, neither in the parish of Brailsford nor in that of Osmaston, and that no Papist hath any concern in either of them . . . Samuel Labonneil, rector.

26. BRAMPTON

26 June 1705: Nil Return. Francis Littlewood, curate; Francis Owtrem, John Roberts, churchwardens.

1706: Nil Returns. Peter Littlewood, curate.

27. BRASSINGTON

28 June 1705: Nil Return. William Alsopp, Ralph Johnson, churchwardens.

1706: No Return.

28. BREADSALL

22 Nov. 1705: Nil Return. Gilbert Michell, rector.

4 Oct. 1706: These are to certify your lordship that there is neither any Papist nor reputed Papist dwelling within the parish of Breadsall in the county of Derby, and that the advowson or right of presentation to the church is not in the disposition of any Papist or reputed Papist or of any other in trust for any such person, and that there is not any school founded within the parish. Gilbert Michell.

29. BRETBY

28 June 1705: Nil Return. William Brown, curate; Thomas Willson, churchwarden.
1706: No Return.

30. BRIMINGTON

8 Nov. 1705: Nil Return. John Peck, vicar of Chesterfield.

1706: No Return.

31. BUXTON, CHELMORTON AND SHELDON

27 Jan. 1707: Nil Return. Thomas Wilson, vicar of Bakewell.

32. CALDWELL

28 June 1705: Nil Return. George Coulton, churchwarden.

1706: **See 148.**

33. CARSINGTON

28 June 1705: Nil Return. Samuel Hutchinson, Robert Needham, churchwardens.

1706: These are to certify whom it may concern that there is neither Papist nor reputed Papist dwelling in our parish: the right of presentation of our church is not in the disposition of any Papist or reputed Papist nor of any other in trust for any such person. We have no school founded by any one within our parish. Samuel Brough, rector; Samuel Hutchinson and Robert Needham, churchwardens.

34. CASTLETON AND EDALE

14 Nov. 1705: Nil Return. Thomas Roe, vicar.

35. CASTLETON

2 Oct. 1706: There is no Papist nor reputed Papist that I know of dwelling within my parish, nor is the advowson of my church in the disposition of any such. We have no school. Thomas Roe, vicar.

36. CHADDESDEN

28 June 1705: Nil Return. Samuel Fletcher, curate; George Goodwin and William Crickly, chapelwardens.

1706: See 142.

37. CHAPEL EN LE FRITH*

16 Nov. 1705: The Papists or reputed Papists in the parish of Chapel en le Frith . . . are as follows: Thomas Kyrke of Hoslheads (Hallsteads?) about £5 or £6 per annum; Henry Kyrke of Eaves about £10 per annum; William Kyrke, shoemaker; Matthew Roebuck, pauper. Caleb Cooke, curate.

1706: My lord in pursuance of your letter I have made all the scrutiny can be and have herein sent your lordship a true account of all the Papists or reputed Papists and their qualities, estates and places of abode within my said parish of Chapel en le Frith as followeth: Henry Kirk of Eaves, land of inheritance about £18 or £20 per annum; Thomas Kirk and Henry Kirk, his son, of Hosled (Hallsteads?) land of inheritance betwixt them about £10 or £12 per annum; Matthew Rawback, shoemaker, a pauper, which four are all in the said parish and none of them have any donation of anything belonging to any church, chapel or free school in the parish or elsewhere. Caleb Cooke.

38. CHELLASTON

28 June 1705: Nil Return. Henry Smith, curate; Henry Meakin and William Martin. churchwardens.

1706: Nil Return. Henry Smith, minister.

39. CHELMORTON

18 No. 1705: Nil Return. James Hulme, minister or curate.

1706: See 31.

40. CHESTERFIELD

26 June 1705: We have but one Papist or reputed Papist in Chesterfield whose name is John Dixon, a singleman: we do not know of any estate he hath, which is all of any degree or quality whatsoever. Godfrey Spencer, John Bretland, churchwardens.

Oct. 1706: A true account of the Papists and reputed Papists in the parish of Chesterfield aforesaid: We have John Dixon, a singleman, who hath no real estate which we know of, but rents an estate of about £20 per annum. We have also one John Lenton, a married man, a gardener, who hath no estate as we know of besides his few household goods. Neither our church nor school nor chapel are in the disposition or donation of any Papist or reputed Papist or any person in trust for them. John Peck, vicar.

41. CHURCH BROUGHTON

28 June 1705: Nil Return. Thomas Manlove, curate; Edward Hurd and Thomas Turner, churchwardens.

18 Oct. 1706: Nil Return. Thomas Manlove, vicar.

42. CHURCH GRESLEY

28 June 1705: Nil Return. John Rath and John Choyes.

26 Sept. 1706: This is humble to certify that there is neither Papist nor reputed Papist in the parish of Gresley, nor is the donation of the church in the disposition of any Papist or reputed Papist. There is no school. John Cary, curate.

43. CLOWNE

26 June 1705: There are no Papists or reputed Papists within our parish except Anne Hides, widow, who keeps a victualling house, and Elizabeth, the wife of John Shepherd, labourer. Charles Basseldine, Joseph Richardson, churchwardens.

9 Oct. 1706: An account of the Papists within the parish of Clowne in the county of Derby: Anne Hides, widow; Elizabeth, the wife of John Shephard, labourer. No Papist hath right of presentation to our church nor any school within our parish. George Chantry, rector.

44. CRICH

28 June 1705: Nil Return. Thomas England, vicar; William Nightingale and Christopher Silvester, churchwardens.

11 Oct. 1706: Nil Return. Thomas England, curate.

45. CROXALL

1705: Nil Return. John Daniel, vicar.
26 July 1706: Nil Return. John Daniel, vicar.

46. CUBLEY

1705: Papists in the parish of Cubley are these: John Hall, shoemaker, Francis Hall, shoemaker. John Proudman, curate.

47. CUBLEY AND MARSTON MONTGOMERY

5 Oct. 1706: Papists and reputed Papists in the parish of Cubley are these following: John Hall and Joan, his wife, papists: he is a shoemaker and rents £15 a year; Henry the son of John Hall aforesaid, husbandman, a Papist. He lives with his father. Francis Hall (a poor labourer), a reputed Papist. At Marston Montgomery there are no Papists except Mary, the wife of John Wood (a shoemaker), who is so reputed. Neither the advowson nor any school in either of the said parishes is in the disposition of any Papist or reputed Papist nor in any person in trust for them. John Proudman, curate.

48. DALBURY

1705: Nil Return. Francis Harris, curate.

1706: These are to certify to your lordship that we have no Papists nor reputed Papists within our parish, that the presentation of our rectory is not in the hands of any such persons in trust and that we have no school, hospital etc at all. Francis Harris, curate.

49. DALE ABBEY*

1705: These are to certify that there is one Robert Needham and William Shaw that are Papists of Dale Abbey . . . which is all the Papists or reputed Papists in the said town of Dale Abbey. John Bogwell, churchwarden.

1706: No Return.

50. DARLEY DALE

23 June 1705: Nil Return. Henry Aldrich, rector.

30 Sept. 1706: This may certify your lordship that in the parish of Darley in the county of Derby there is no Papist nor reputed Papist, and that the presentation to the church of Darley aforesaid belongs to the Reverend the Dean of Lincoln for the time being, and that the ministers, churchwardens and overseers of the poor of Darley for the time being are intrusted for the school. Henry Aldrich, rector.

51. DENBY

28 June 1705: Nil Return. William Taylor, vicar; Vincent Fletcher and Robert Cresswell, churchwardens.

1706: No Return.

52. DERBY, ALL SAINTS

28 June 1705: There is one woman, the wife of Henry Thorpe, barber, of Derby, a Papist of no estate, which is all the Papists or reputed Papists within our parish. Francis Walker, Samuel Cooke, churchwardens.

1706: There is one Papist or reputed Papist, Anne, the wife of Henry Thorpe, a poor woman, in the parish of All Saints in Derby and no more: the presentation of our church is not in any Papist or reputed Papist nor in any person in trust for them. We have not any school founded in our parish. Walter Horton.

53. DERBY, ST. ALKMUND

28 June 1705: Nil Return. W. Hodgkinson, Francis Jones, churchwardens.

1706: There is not one Papist or reputed Papist in the parish of St. Alkmund in Derby: the presentation of our church is not in any Papist or reputed Papist nor in any person in trust for them. We have not any school founded in our parish.

54. DERBY, ST. MICHAEL

28 June 1705: Nil Return. George Buxton, Benjamin Sales, churchwardens.

1706: No Return.

55. DERBY, ST. PETER

28 June 1705: Nil Return. William Osborn, vicar; Ralph Skampton and Martin Tompson, churchwardens.

56. DERBY, ST. PETER AND NORMANTON BY DERBY

1706: There is neither Papist nor reputed Papist that we know of within the parish of St. Peter's in the town of Derby nor chapelry of Normanton. The present incumbent, William Osborne, was nominated to the vicarage by the Corporation of Derby but presented by the worshipful family of the Dixies of (Market) Bosworth in Leicestershire, in which family the right of presentation, we believe, now is by agreement with the Corporation of Derby. There is a free school within the parish of St. Peter's at the disposal of the Corporation of Derby. William Osborne, vicar; Gilbert Wagstaff, churchwarden.

57. DERBY, ST. WERBURGH

28 June 1705: Nil Return. James Walker, vicar; William Lord and Richard Alleyne, churchwardens.

1706: I do certify that as far as I know there is no Papist or reputed Papist in my parish; that the advowson of the vicarage is in the Crown; that there is no school endowed. James Walker, vicar.

58. DOVERIDGE

28 June 1705 Nil Return. William Palmer jnr, John Palmer, churchwardens.

27 Sept. 1706: I do hereby certify that there's no Papist nor reputed Papist of any quality or estate or abode within the parish of Doveridge in the county of Derby (only there's an annuity of £220 payed by Godfrey Clark, Esq., to Mrs. Noll in the county of Hereford or Gloucester, widow, durng the rest of her natural life). And I do certify that there's no advowson nor right of presentation nor donation of any church nor any schoo! founded in the aforesaid parish in the disposition of any Papists or reputed Papists or of any other in trust for any such person. Luke Glenn, vicar.

59. DRONFIELD*

1705: The names of the Papists or popishly affected in the parish of Dronfield and county of Derby. **Dronfield Quarter:** Vincent Eyre and his wife, gentleman, per annum £40, Woodhouse; Henry Woomack and his wife, skinner, O, Dronfield; William Steel, blacksmith, 0, Dronfield; **Coal Aston and Unston Quarter:** Katherine Billam, widow, per annum £4, Coal Aston Moor; **Holmesfield Quarter:** Robert Wostenholm and wife, gentleman decayed in estate, Morewood (now in prison); Fanshaw Wostenholme, his son, O, Morewood; Ignatius Woomack and wife, glover, O, Morewood; Christian Hattersley, widow, O, Holmesfield; **Dore Quarter:** Robert Watson, button maker, O, Dore. Christopher Colliss, vicar; Robert Ellis, William Adamson, Richard Downes and Robert Fisher, churchwardens.

1706: An exact account of the Papists or reputed Papists dwelling in the parish of Dronfield in the county of Derby with their qualities, estates and places of abode. Vincent Eyre and wife, gentleman, £40 per annum, Dronfield Woodhouse; Anne More, spinster, Dronfield Woodhouse; Henry Womack, skinner, Dronfield; William Steele, smith, Dronfield; Mary Allen, spinster, Dronfield; Robert Fox, mason, Coal Aston. **Holmesfield Lordship:** Robert Wolstenholme snr, and Fan(shaw) Wolstenholme, jnr, yeomen, £20 per annum, Dronfield Woodhouse; Ignatius Womack, skinner, Morewood; Christian Hattersley, spinster, Holmesfield; **Dore:** Robert Watson, button maker, Dore; George Marshall, smelter, Totley Bents. The patrons of the church and school are neither Papists nor popishly affected. Christopher Collice, vicar; W. Frith, Thomas Barker, Timothy Atkin, Robert Fisher, churchwardens.

60. DUFFIELD

28 June 1705: There is one Lunt and his wife now liveth in this parish, both Papists, but they being strangers we do not know of what quality they are of, which is all the Papists within our parish. John Harrison, John Steene, churchwardens.

1706: Nil Return. Joseph Gorwey, vicar.

61. ECKINGTON*

9 Nov. 1705: These are to certify whom it may concern that in the parish of Eckington in the county of Derby and diocese of Lichfield and Coventry are these Papists or reputed Papists following: John Pole, esquire, of Spinkhill and his wife, his estate is reckoned about £300 per annum; also one Piercy, a reputed priest, supposed to live in Mr. Pole's family; Francis Sikes; Elias Syddall; Richard Harwood; Christopher Thorpe; Michael Priest; Cecily Browne, widow; William Wilcockson; Richard Eely; Margaret Clay; George Hobson, senior; George Hobson, junior; two daughters of William Hobson's lately deceased; all these poor ones; Mr. Marshal, his estate about £18 per anuum; William Ellis, his estate about £12 per annum; Francis Boston; all these of Spinkhill; George Savage of the Haven, his estate about £15 or £16 per annum; George Hobson, his estate about £12 per annum; George Staniforth of Jeere Lane (Geer Lane), his estate about £35 per annum. This is the best account I can at present give. Samuel Gardiner, rector.

62. ECKINGTON AND KILLAMARSH*

1706: Papists dwelling in the parish of Eckington cum Killamarsh: John Pole, esquire, about £300 per annum in this parish and elsewhere in the county; Also one Percy, a priest in his house; George Staniforth of Jeer Lane (Geer Lane) £30 per annum; George Howson of Ridgeway £9; George Savage of the Haven £16; John Marshal of Spinkhill £18; William Ellis of Spinkhill £9; William Wilcockson, George Hobson snr, George Hobson jnr, Michael Priest, Christopher Thorpe, Francis Sikes, Richard Ely, Richard Harwood, Elias Sydall, Francis Boston, William Selby, all of Spinkhill worth 0; Roger Barker of the Slitting Mill worth 0; Gabriel Boston, rent about £18 per annum; Robert Wilcockson, about £3 per annum estate; Joseph Cheetham, Anne Lolly, Widow Cheetham, Joseph Hawworth, all worth 0; John Ely of Eckington worth 0. No Papist nor reputed Papist has any right of presentation to this church or of donation of any school in this parish or any other in trust for any such person, nor in Kilmarsh. Samuel Gardiner, rector.

63. EDENSOR*

26 June 1705: The certificate of the minister and churchwardens of Edensor in the county of Derby pursuant to an order of the Queen and Council is as follows: That there is one Michael Sherwood, a Papist in the parish of Edensor, a poor man. John Griffiths, curate; John Salt and John Woodhouse, churchwardens.

10 Dec. 1706: These are to certify your lordship that there is no Papist or reputed Papist within our parish of Edensover. The donation of the church is in the gift of His Grace the Duke of Devonshire, who is no Papist, and, as for a school, we have none founded in our parish. John Griffith, curate.

64. EDALE

1705: See 34.

29 Sept. 1706: I, William Street, curate of Edale in the parish of Castleton in the county of Derby do hereby . . . certify there is not any Papist or reputed Papist dwelling within the said chapelry. As also that the advowson . . . of the said chapel is not in the disposition of any Papist or reputed Papist or any other in trust for such person. And school there is none founded in the chapelry. William Street.

65. EDLASTON

6 Nov. 1705: Nil Return. Samuel Smalley, curate.

20 Sept. 1706: I do hereby certify that there is no Papist or reputed Papist within the parish of Edlaston and that the advowson or right of presentation is not in the disposition of any Papist or reputed Papist nor in any person in trust for any such person. We have no school in our parish. Samuel Smalley, curate.

66. EGGINTON

1705: These are to certify that in the parish of Egginton we have only two Papists reputed, William Lisle and his wife aged near fourscore, inconsiderable, poor people. J. Beardsley, rector.

4 Oct. 1706: These are to certify that in the town and parish of Egginton there are two Papists, viz. William Lisle and his wife, inconsiderable persons. He has been servant to the late Sir Henry Every, and what he maintains himself by is some skill he pretends to in surgery. They are aged near eighty years. I also certify the advowson or right of presentation of the rectory is in Protestant hands, viz. Sir Henry Every and Mr. Pole of Radbourne. I also certify we have no schools founded in our parish. John Beardsley, rector.

67. ELMTON

7 Nov. 1705: Nil Return. John Davenport, vicar.

1 Oct. 1706: These are to certify you that there are neither Papists nor reputed Papists within the parish of Elmton. The right of presentation of the Church is not in the disposition of any Papist or reputed Papist There is not any school founded in the parish. John Davenport, vicar.

68. ELTON

26 June 1705: Nil Return. Thomas Prince, curate; Thomas Beard and William Halley, chapelwardens.

2 Oct. 1706: Nil Return. Thomas Prince, curate.

69. ELVASTON

8 Dec. 1705: Nil Return. Anthony Blackwell, vicar.

4 Oct. 1706: There is not one Papist or reputed Papist in the church of Elvaston in the county of Derby. The advowson or right of presentation of that church is not in the disposition of any Papist or reputed Papist or in any other in trust for any such person. There is no school in that parish. Anthony Blackwall, vicar.

70. ETWALL

28 June 1705: Nil Return. Ellis Cunliffe.

3 July 1706: These are to certify that there are no Papists or reputed Papists residing in the parish abovesaid; nor does the advowson or right of presentation to the church of Etwall belong to any Papist or reputed Papist or to any person in trust for them. We have no school founded in our parish. Ellis Cunliffe, vicar.

71. EYAM

1705: No Return.

2 Oct. 1706: A true and perfect account of all Papists and reputed Papists in the parish of Eyam in the county of Derby delivered in at the probate court held at Chesterfield in the said county of Derby the 2nd day of October . . . 1706: Anne, the wife of William Stone of Eyam, Papist, pauper, and William Stone, her husband, reputed Papist; John Torr and Mary, his wife, of Leam in the parish of Eyam, yeoman freeholder of ten pounds a year and upwards; Henry Hunter and Anne, his wife, reputed Papists, paupers. The presentation of the church is in the hand of no Papist nor any in trust for them. No school we have. Joseph Hunter, rector; Richard Brightmore, William Fearn, Thomas Drable, Thomas Morton, churchwardens.

72. FAIRFIELD

16 Nov. 1705: Nil Return. Edward Hollinshead, curate.

1706: No Return.

73. FENNY BENTLEY

28 June 1705: Nil Return. Luke Flint, curate; William Smith, churchwarden.

1706: No Return.

74. FINDERN

30 Nov. 1705: Nil Return. John Ward, vicar of Mickleover.

1706: See 106.

75. FOREMARK

28 June 1705: Nil Return. Richard Fowler, curate; Henry Ferne, churchwarden.

1706: See 128.

76. GLOSSOP*

1705: We have no Papists nor reputed Papists within the parish.
William Bagshaw, vicar. Memorandum: My Lord George Howard of Norfolk, a reputed Papist, is the patron of Glossop.

30 Sept. 1706: In pursuance to your commands this comes to inform you that there is no Papist nor reputed Papist in my parish that I know of, and, as for the right of presentation of the vicarage of Glossop, it is in the disposal of Henry St. George, knight, Charles Mawson, esquire and Thomas Barker, gentleman, trustees for my Lord George Howard of Norfolk, who, I believe, may be a reputed Papist. As to the school at Glossop it is in the gift of my Lord George Howard's trustees; and the family of the Norfolks, (or whoever else was possessed of the manor of Glossop) always gave £10 per annum to the school of Glossop as a gratuity, but we have nothing to show for it. But there is thirty shillings by the year belonging to Glossop School, which was left by a pious and charitable person about eight years ago for the encouragement of learning. William Bagshaw, vicar.

77. HARTSHORNE

28 June 1705: We, the churchwardens of Hartshorne . . . do hereby certify that we have no Papist or reputed Papist within our parish save only Hatton, the wife of Thomas Hatton, whose husband is a poor man. William Taylor, John Gamble, churchwardens.

3 Oct. 1706: In obedience to your lordship's commands I hereby certify that there is no Papist or reputed Papist in my parish except one woman, very poor and going from us to another place: neither have we any benefits, presentations or any donative of our church or school in the hands of any Papist or reputed Papist, nor in the hands of any in trust for them. Thomas Desborough, rector; William Taylor and John Gamble, churchwardens.

78. HATHERSAGE*

14 Nov. 1705: An Account of the Papists or reputed Papists in the parish of Hathersage . . . George Eyre, £20 per annum; Thomas Eyre, £16 per annum; William Walkden grocer; John Morton, blacksmith; John Cooper, farmer; Thomas Eyre, shoemaker; George Smilter, £10 per annum; John Smilter, tailor; John Cam, tailor; Thomas Ibutson, millstone-maker; Matthew Willcockson, millstone-maker; John Littlewood, mason; Francis Willcoxon, millstone-maker; Thomas Littlewood; Thomas Furnace, farmer; Robert Hinch, miller; Ellice Furnace; Robert Frost, pauper; John Brownel, baker; Samuel Morstin, farmer; Joseph Willcoxen, shoemaker; Matthew Willcoxen; Thomas Willcoxen. p. Alex Hamilton, vicar.

1706: No Return.

79. HAYFIELD

1705: Nil Return. John Sales, curate.

2 Sept. 1706: These are to certify whom it may concern that I, John Sale, curate of Hayfield, have made diligent search and enquiry (according to command) throughout our whole chapelry of Hayfield for Papists or reputed Papists dwelling amongst us, but have not found any; neither is the advowson or right of presentation or donation of our church or chapel or of our school within our chapelry in the disposition of any Papist or reputed Papist or of any other in trust for any such persons. John Sale, curate.

80. HEAGE

1705: Nil Return. Joseph Gorwey, vicar of Duffield.

1706: No Return.

81. HEANOR*

28 June 1705: An exact account of all the Papists or reputed Papists within the parish of Heanor . . . exhibited at a court held at Derby 28 June 1705: There is only in this parish one reputed Papist viz. Mr. Charles Low, the place of whose abode is Oldgrave (Algrave) within the parish of Heanor, and his estate is valued by the neighbourhood at £40 per annum. William Greatorex, curate.

4 Oct. 1706: A list of the Papists or reputed Papists in the parish of Heanor in the county of Derby and diocese of Lichfield together with an account of their qualities, estates and places of abode, delivered in at the probate court held at Derby by the right worshipful William Walmsley, Chancellor of the diocese of Lichfield and Coventry aforesaid or his deputy on the 4th day of October Anno Domini 1706: Mr. Charles Low, gentleman, about £47 per annum, lives at Owlgreaves (Algrave) in the parish of Heanor aforesaid; Widow Shaw, pauper, lives at Shipley Wood in the parish aforesaid. Our church is not in the donation of any Papist or reputed Papist nor of any entrusted for them that I know or believe. We have no free school in the parish. William Greatorex, curate.

82. HEATH

30 June 1705: Nil Return. Edward Revell, rector; John Mosley and Jonathan Bacon, churchwardens.

30 Sept. 1706: A true and exact account of all the Papists and reputed Papists in the parish of Heath alias Lownde in the county of Derby and whether any Papist or reputed Papist hath our advowson or right of presentation to our church or donation of any school or estate in our parish: George Hobson, a poor servant, pauper. We have no school in our parish, nor hath any Papist or reputed Papist our advowson or right of presentation, neither is there any estate in our parish belonging to any Papist or reputed Papist. Edward Revell, rector.

83. HOGNASTON

28 June 1705: Nil Return. Anthony Holmes, churchwarden.

1706: No Return.

84. HOPE

8 Oct. 1705: My Lord: This, in obedience to your lordship's command is to acquaint you that there are in the parish of Hope in the county of Derby these following Roman Catholics, viz: In the Woodland Mrs. Mary Eyre and her mother, substantial tenants; the wife of Samuel Greaves, a substantial tenant, in the same place; Widow Barber and her daughter of the same place, a poor tenant; Jacob Ashton of Hope, a man of about £10 per annum; two Widow Slacks, one of Hope and the other of Bradwell, both poor widows; and one Mrs. Straley at the windmill, who maintains herself by teaching a small school. These are all that I know of and is all at present. J. Cresswell.

7 Oct. 1706: In obedience to your lordship's commands I have made what scrutiny I could to find out all Papists or reputed Papists there are within my parish and I can find only these following viz: The wife of Joseph Eyre of Cockbridge, a husbandman and tenant who rents about £20 a year; Mary Barber of Birchinlee and her (?daughter) . . . a year but poor; Thomas Frost but poor in Wood(lands) . . .; Samuel Greaves and his wife of Woodland a . . . who rents about £40 a year; the wife of Gilbert Marshall of Woodland, about £10 a year; Mrs. Mary Bagnall formerly Mrs. Mary Eyre, substantial tenant who rents about £80 per annum . . . husband had or where his estate is I cannot . . . think in Lincolnshire; Jacob Ashton of Hope who has about £10 per annum; Widow Slack of Bradwell; Thomas Willcockson, a substantial tenant who rents about £20 a year. The advowson or right of presentation or donation of our church or any other or of any school either in my parish or in any other, none of these are at their disposal or be at the disposition of any other in trust for any of them. J. Cresswell.

85. ILKESTON

28 June 1705: Nil Return. Joseph Cocker, Philip Atkin, churchwardens.

1706: See 145.

86. HORSLEY

28 June 1705: There is within our parish Charles Alcock and Dorothy Fouke which are Papists. They are poor people, which are all the Papists or reputed Papists within our parish. William Taylor, vicar; Luke Abbot and Henry Brown, churchwardens.

1706: No Return.

87. KEDLESTON

28 June 1705: Nil Return. George Souter, William Tantum, churchwardens.

4 Oct. 1706: We have neither Papist nor reputed Papist in our parish. The rectory is in the donation of neither Papist nor reputed Papist nor any person in trust for any such. Neither have we any school in our parish. Thomas Wright, rector.

88. KILLAMARSH

9 Nov. 1705: The Papists or reputed Papists of Killamarsh . . . are as follows: Robert Wilcock, £3 per annum; John Hanworth, labourer; Widow Lolly, Widow Chetham, paupers. John Stephenson, curate.

1706: See 62.

89. KIRK HALLAM

28 June 1705: Nil Return. Michael Boswell, Richard Birch, churchwardens.

1706: Nil Return. Edward Folley, curate; Henry Burton and Joseph Walker, churchwardens.

90. KIRK IRETON

28 June 1705: Nil Return. Samuel Moore, rector; Samuel Toplis and William Haynes, churchwardens.

9 Sept. 1706; Nil Return. Samuel Mower, rector.

91. KIRK LANGLEY

28 June 1705: Nil Return. Thomas Meynell, rector; Richard Parker and John Windley snr, churchwardens.

1706: No Return.

92. KNIVETON*

1705: That there is but one Papist abiding in the parish of Kniveton aforesaid, his name is William Tipper, a mean man, that hath no estate of his own, but rents a small tenement from year to year which may perhaps keep 4 or 5 cows. His wife is a Protestant, but he hath four small children, three boys and a girl which (as we suppose) are all baptised after the way of the Church of Rome. Isaac Greatorex, minister.

8 Oct. 1706: My Lord: According to the commands of his heart, the Archbishop of Canterbury and your lordship's I make bold to acquaint your lordship that there is but one Papist an inhabitant in the parish of Kniveton in the county of Derby, a very ordinary and ignorant man and, being formerly a servant in a Papist's family, he was perverted by them. He is a husbandman by calling and holds some little land in the said parish upon a rack rent; his wife is a Protestant of the Church of England; and he hath four small children which, I suppose, are baptised after the way of the Church of Rome, for they were not brought to our church. The donation of the said church of Kniveton is not in the hands of any Papist or reputed Papist, nor is there any school founded in the said parish. Isaac Greatorex, vicar.

93. LANGWITH

28 June 1705: Nil Return. John Newton, rector.

30 Sept. 1706: These are to certify that there is neither Papist nor reputed Papist within the parish of Over Langwith in the county of Derby. Neither is there any school founded in the said parish. The Right Noble the Duke of Devonshire is lord of the town and patron of the church. John Newton, rector.

94. LITTLEOVER

28 June 1705: Nil Return. John Moxon, Edward Holden, chapelwardens.

1706. See 105.

95. LONGFORD

1705: The names of the Papists and reputed Papists within the parish of Longford: Thomas Brandon, pauper in the almshouse, of Longford; Alice, wife of Thomas Brown junior of Bentley, gentleman; Anne, wife of George Harris of Alkmanton, pauper; Widow Pole of Bentley, gentlewoman. Luke Budworth, vicar.

1706: The names etc of all the Papists or reputed Papists within the parish of Longford: Alice, wife of Thomas Brown junior of Bentley, gentleman; Elizabeth Pole of the same, widow; Anne Gosling of the same, gentlewoman; Ralph Falkaner of the same, cordwainer, and Anne, his wife; Anne, wife of George Harris of Alkmanton, pauper; Grace, wife of John Cooper of the same, pauper; Thomas Brandon of Longford, pauper; Anne Brandon of the same, spinster. There is no free school in our parish. The advowson or right of presentation of our church, neither rectory nor vicarage, belongs to any Papist or reputed Papist nor to any one in trust for any such person. Luke Budworth, vicar.

7 Oct. Sir: The advowson of our parish not being in Papists' hands I thought it needless to insert any thing about it when I sent an account of the Papists in my parish to Derby by my churchwardens on Friday last. But since you would not accept it without that was put in I have done according to your orders. Luke Budworth.

96. LONGSTONE

1705: Nil Return. Samuel Mills, curate.

1706: Nil Return. Samuel Mills, curate.

97. LULLINGTON

1705: Nil Return. William Tavenar, Richard Sheperd, churchwardens.

26 Sept. 1706: I have humbly presumed to certify whom it may concern that there is no Papist in my parish nor any to my knowledge suspected such, and that the perpetual donation of the vicarage of Lullington aforesaid is in the sole dispose of the crown of England, and that there is not any free school or other in the said parish but a private grammar school that has nothing of free gift belonging to the same. Joseph Smith, vicar.

98. MACKWORTH

12 Nov. 1705: Nil Return. Jasper Horsington, vicar; William Mumford and Joshua Dawson, churchwardens.

99. MACKWORTH, ALLESTREE AND QUARNDON

1705: See 2 and 98.

4 Oct. 1706: Nil Rteurn. Jasper Horsington.

100. MARSTON UPON DOVE

28 June 1705: Nil Return. Richard Wilkes, Edward Evans, churchwardens.

5 Oct. 1705: Nil Return. George Gretton, vicar.

4 Oct. 1706: Nil Return. George Gretton, vicar.

101. MARSTON MONTGOMERY

28 June 1705: I, Thomas Townsend, churchwarden of Marston Montgomery, do present John Leash of Marston Montgomery aforesaid . . . to be a reputed Papist but hath no lands or tenements. Thomas Townsend, churchwarden.

1706: See 47.

102. MATLOCK

1705: Nil Return. Joseph Fern, rector; John Smith and William Bunting, churchwardens.

2 Oct. 1706: These may further certify that we have not in our parish of Matlock in the county of Derby any either Papist or reputed Papist residing amongst us: as also that the presentation to our parish church and nomination to our school belongs not to any Papist or reputed Papist, but the former to the Reverend the Dean of Lincoln, the latter to the minister and churchwardens for the time being and the heirs of Mr. George Spateman. Joseph Fern, rector.

103. MEASHAM

28 June 1705: Nil Return. John Perkins, curate; William Hill and George Nurse, churchwardens.

26 Sept. 1706: This is humbly to certify there is neither Papist nor reputed Papist in the parish of Measham, nor is the donation of the curacy in the disposition of any Papist or reputed Papist. There is no school. John Cary, curate.

104. MELBOURNE

28 June 1705: Nil Return. John Wrangleton; Samuel Symes and George Peate, churchwardens.

29 Sept. 1706: This is to certify that the Papists (or so reputed) in the parish of Melbourne in the county of Derby are viz: Elizabeth, the wife of John Harrison, fidler; Widow Clifford and Elizabeth Rolson, two poor women, and that there are no more that I know of. I do further certify that there is no advowson or right of presentation or donation of our church or of any school founded in our said parish by any Papist or reputed Papist nor of any other in trust for any such person. John Troughton, vicar.

105. MELLOR

26 June 1705: Nil Return. William Street, curate.

9 Oct. 1706: Sir: As we came to the visitation to Chesterfield Mr. Sales of Hayfield gave us my Lord's letter together with the Order of Council requiring our minister to give an exact account of the number of Papists and reputed Papists dwelling within our parish at the probate court, but the probate court being over before we received the order we could not answer it. By whose neglect it was miscarried we cannot tell, but upon receipt thereof we thought it our duty to certify to my Lord that we have no Papists within our chapelry nor any advowson or right of presentation or donation of the chapel or of any school founded within our liberty or chapelry in the disposition of any Papist or reputed Papist or of any other in trust for any such person. William Hambleton, William Wood, chapelwardens. We had no minister at Mellor 'till last Sunday since May last.

106. MICKLEOVER

1705: Nil Return. Abraham Handley, William Hawood, churchwardens.

4 Oct. 1706: After strict examination and enquiry I do not find or know of any Papists or reputed Papists living or residing within the liberty or parish of Mickleover or within either of its two members viz. the chapelries of Littleover and

Findern. The advowson or right of presentation to the church of Over alias Mickleover is not in the disposition of any Papist or reputed Papist or of any other person in trust for them. There is no school or hospital founded within the said parish of Over or any of its members. John Ward, vicar.

107. MONYASH

19 Nov. 1705: Nil Return. John Howman, John Rotlif, chapelwardens.

4 Oct. 1706: Nil Return. John Mills, curate.

108. MORLEY

28 June 1705: Nil Return. William Holland, Edward Madin, churchwardens.

4 Oct. 1706: In obedience to your lordship's command I certify your lordship that there is neither Papist nor reputed Papist in the parish of Morley, nor is the advowson or right of presentation of my church in the disposition of any Papist or reputed Papist or of any other in trust for any such person, that there is no school in my parish founded by any person. William Wilson, rector.

109. MORTON

26 June 1705: Nil Return. John Fowles, rector; James Parsons and James Swift, churchwardens.

2 Oct. 1706: We have a poor widow a Roman Catholic in the parish. The advowson of the church belongs to the Lord Scarsdale. We have no school in our parish. Joseph Smith, curate.

110. MUGGINTON

28 June 1705: Nil Return. Richard Poole, vicar; Thomas Beeson, Joseph Johnson and Joseph Barnes, churchwardens.

4 Oct. 1706: These are to certify that in the parish of Mugginton in the county of Derby there is neither Papist nor reputed Papist. Neither is the presentation of the church in the disposition of any Papist or reputed Papist or of any in trust for them. Neither is there any school founded in the same parish. Richard Pole, rector.

111. NEWTON SOLNEY

20 Nov. 1705: Nil Return. Thomas Manlove, minister.

1706: Nil Return. Thomas Manlove, minister.

112. NORBURY★

27 June 1705: An exact account of the names of Papists and reputed Papists and also of their qualities and estates within the parish of Norbury and Roston: William Fitzherbert, esquire, his estate in Norbury and Roston £400 per year; The presentation of Norbury belongs to William Fitzherbert, esquire; Mr. Christopher Adams, his agent; Mr. William Adams; John Mold, his estate £18 per year; William Cooper £1 10s per year; Robert Bill £1 per year; John Oldacre £6 10s per year; Thomas Cope £7 10s per year; Robert Greensmith £1 10s per year; John Bill £4 10s per year; Anthony Greensmith; Laurence Greensmith; Thomas Wood; John Slater; Basil Milnhouse; Nick Palmer; William Palmer, senior; William Palmer, junior; Ignatius Greensmith; Nicholas Harrison; William Cope; Thomas Shirlock; Thomas Smith; Richard Harrison. John Wooley and Benjamin Mossley, churchwardens.

1706: A list of the Papists or reputed Papists of Norbury and Roston in the county of Derby with their respective qualities, estates and places of abode: William Fitzherbert, esquire, of West Chester £618 per annum; Mr. Christopher Adams, his agent at Norbury, Mr. William Adams at Norbury, his son, their estates at Marston Montgomery; John Mold per annum of Roston £15 15s; William Cooper per annum of Roston £1 10s; Robert Bill of Roston £10; John Oldacre of Roston £6 15s; Thomas Cope, senior, of Roston £7 10s; Ignatius Greensmith of Roston £2; John Bill of Norbury per annum £4 10s; Constance Harrison of Roston, a minor, £3; John Slater of Roston 0; Basil Palmer of Roston 0. These estates are valued according to the levies which I judged the best method : The advowson belongs to William Fitzherbert, esquire, but I was presented by my father-in-law Sir Simon Degge (deceased). The next presentation is to Mr. Luke Budworth, the vicar of Longford in this county, Mr. Ralph Docksey of Snelston in trust for it. We have a school founded in our parish, the disposition whereof is not in any Papist or reputed Papist nor any other person in trust for them. A. Trollope, rector. Mr. Christopher's and Mr. William Adam's estate lying in the parish of Marston Montgomery £50 p.a., but I can't learn how it is divided. A school founded within the parish but not by a Papist or reputed Papist.

113. NORMANTON BY DERBY

28 June 1705: Nil Return. Samuel Pegg, George Stenson, churchwardens.
1706: See 55.

114. NORTH WINGFIELD

26 June 1706: Nil Return. John Lee, curate; Thomas Fidlar and John Hobson, churchwardens.
2 Oct. 1706: Nil Return. Matthew Powel, rector.

115. NORTON

9 Nov. 1705: Nil Return. Samuel Trickett, vicar.
26 Sept. 1706: These are to certify . . . that we have no Papists or reputed Papists within the parish of Norton in the county of Derby excepting Katherine, the wife of Francis Warrington of Greenhill in the parish of Norton who is a carpenter and who comes to our church, but his wife is a Papist, and a daughter she had by a former husband, whose name is Elizabeth Billam, a girl of about eight or nine years of age, whom the mother brings up a Papist. The advowson or right of presentation or donation of our church, benefice or school are not in the disposition of any Papist or reputed Papist nor any in trust for them, but those that are patrons both of church and school are persons that are firm for the Church of England as it is established by law. Samuel Trickett, vicar.

116. OCKBROOK AND SANDIACRE

28 June 1705: Nil Return. Stephen Grongnet, vicar of Ockbrook and curate of Sandiacre.
3 Oct. 1706: Nil Return. Stephen Grongnet.

117. OSMASTON BY DERBY, ALVASTON AND BOULTON

12 Nov. 1705: Nil Return. Hugh Broome, minister.

118. OSMASTON BY DERBY

4 Oct. 1706: Nil Return. Hugh Broome, curate.

119. OSMASTON BY ASHBOURNE

28 June 1705: We, the churchwardens of Osmaston juxta Ashbourne in the county of Derby, do certify that we have no Papists within us but Thomas Oldacres who is a tenant within us, holds about £10 or £15 per annum. Humphrey Pegg, John Hewson, churchwardens.
1706: See 25.

120. PARWICH

28 June 1705: Nil Return. Thomas Johnson, curate.

3 Oct. 1706: Nil Return. Thomas Johnson, curate.

121. PEAK FOREST

10 Nov. 1705: Nil Return. William Oldfield, curate.

1706: I have made a scrutiny in our precinct and find two reputed Papists, Thomas Longdor, Ralph Lomas, men of none estates. As to our church it is a donative from the Duke of Devonshire, neither have we any founded school. William Oldfield, S. Wharley.

122. PENTRICH

28 June 1705: Nil Return. William Licet, vicar; Richard Richardson and William Robin, churchwardens.

23 August 1706: There is neither Papist nor reputed Papist within the said parish, and the right of presentation to the said vicarage is in the Most Noble His Grace the Duke of Devonshire, and that we have no school founded within the said parish. William Licett.

123. PINXTON

26 June 1705: Nil Return. John Malton, George Hodkinson, churchwardens.

1706: There is no Papist or reputed Papist within the parish of Pinxton . . . and that the advowson, right of presentation or donation of our church is wholly in the power of honest gentlemen, being born sons of the Church of England. We have no free school here. Richard Rayner, rector.

124. PLEASLEY

25 June 1705: Nil Return. Henry Chapell, rector.

1 Oct. 1706: These are to certify: 1. There is no Papist or reputed Papist dwelling within the parish of Pleasley aforesaid. 2. That there is no school foundation in the said parish. 3. That the advowson or right of presentation to the church of Pleasley aforesaid is not in the disposition of any Papists or reputed Papists or any other in trust for any Papist or reputed Papist. Henry Chappell, rector.

125: RADBOURNE

1705: Nil Return. Francis Ward, rector.

1706: In the parish of Radbourne in the county of Derby I have is neither Papist nor reputed Papist; neither is the presentation of the church in the disposition of any Papist or of any in trust for them; neither is there any school founded in the same parish. Francis Ward, rector.

126. RAVENSTONE

14 Nov. 1705: Nil Return. Thomas Postell, rector.

1706: Nil Return. Thomas Postell, rector.

127. REPTON*

13 Nov. 1705: Nil Return. Samuel Fowler, minister.

128. REPTON AND FOREMARK*

4 Oct. 1706: Nil Return. Samuel Fowler.

10 Oct. 1706: This is to certify whom it may concern that there is no Papist nor reputed Papist that hath any concern about either the parish of Repton or the parish of Foremark; only one Sir William Gerard is one of the governors of the school at Repton jointly with my Lord Huntingdon and my Lord Chester(field). Samuel Fowler, minister.

129. ROSLISTON

28 June 1705: Nil Return. Walter Horton, rector; Francis Moseley, churchwarden.

1706: No Return.

130. SAWLEY AND WILNE

6 Dec. 1705: Nil Return. Samuel Lees, minister; Nathaniel Dodson and Joseph Pimme, churchwardens.

23 Sept. 1706: Nil Return. Francis Coleire, curate.

131. SCARCLIFFE

26 June 1705: There is but one reputed Papist in our parish viz. Anne, the wife of Francis Jamson, a farmer. Roger Lowde, minister; Edward Whittikar and William Kesteven, churchwardens.

2 Sept. 1706: I, the curate of the parish aforesaid whose name is subscribed, do certify that there is no Papist or reputed Papist in our parish save only Anne, the wife of Francis Jamson, a farmer of £25 a year, and Edmund Hall, her son, and likewise I certify that the right of presentation or donation of our church or school is not in the disposition of any Papist or reputed Papist or of any person in trust for any such person. Roger Lowde, curate.

132. SCROPTON

28 June 1705: Nil Return. Thomas Manlove, vicar; Thomas Sheffield and Robert Clifford, churchwardens.

18 Oct. 1706: Nil Return. Thomas Manlove, minister.

133. SHIRLAND

7 Nov. 1705: Nil Return. William Sleigh, rector.

2 Oct. 1706: We have no Roman Catholics in our parish and the advowson of the church belongs to the Duke of Shrewsbury, the Lord Halifax and the Lord George Howard, who present by turns. The Lord George Howard is a Roman Catholic. There is no school in the parish. William Sleigh, rector.

134. SHIRLEY

28 June 1705: Nil Return. Thomas Catterall, vicar; Richard Hitchcock and William Hudson, churchwardens.

3 Oct. 1706: Nil Return. Thomas Catterall, vicar.

135. SMALLEY

28 June 1705: Nil Return. W. Wilson, rector; Thomas Laneton, churchwarden.

1706: No Return.

136. SMISBY

28 June 1705: Nil Return. John Carey, curate; John Tucker, churchwarden.

26 Sept. 1706: This is humbly to certify that there is neither Papist nor reputed Papist in the parish of Smisby, nor is the donation of the church in the disposition of any Papist or reputed Papist. There is no school. John Cary, curate.

137. SNELSTON

13 Nov. 1705: An account of the Papists and reputed Papists in the parish of Snelston in the county of Derby and of their estates etc: William Cooper and his wife, inhabitants of Snelston, they receive alms from the parish; Anne Coxon, in the town of Snelston, a poor woman; Mr. Fitzherbert, the patron of the living, a Papist, a gentleman of great estate and lives either at London or Wales. Brian Harding, curate.

26 Sept. 1706: An exact and particular account of the number of Papists and reputed Papists dwelling within the parish of Snelston with their qualities, estates, etc: William Cooper, a Papist, he receives alms from the parish; Anne Coxon, a reputed Papist, she is a poor woman. The patron of the church is a Papist, but Mr. Trollope, the rector, will give a more exact account of him than I can give. No school founded in the parish. Brian Harding, curate.

138. SOMERSALL HERBERT

1705: Nil Return. John Ashton, curate.

4 Oct. 1706: There are no Papists or reputed Papists dwelling within the parish of Somersall Herbert. Neither is the advowson or right of presentation or donation of the church, as I do verily believe, in the disposition of any Papist or reputed Papist or any other in trust for such person. There is no school founded within the parish. John Ashton, minister.

139. SOUTH NORMANTON

26 June 1705: Nil Return. Roger Smyth, rector; Thomas Morriss and Richard Johnson, churchwardens.

9 Oct. 1706: These are to certify whom it may concern that I have . . . diligently inquired concerning Papists or so reputed but do not find either sort in the parish. Nor does the presentation of this rectory belong to any such or to any in trust for them. Public school have we none. Thomas Elcocke, rector.

140. SOUTH WINGFIELD

7 Nov. 1705: Nil Return. Francis Hill, vicar.

1 Oct. 1706: This is to inform and satisfy whomsoever it may concern that we have no Papists nor reputed Papists dwelling in our parish of South Wingfield, and that the right of presentation belonging to the church of South Wingfield is not in the disposal of any Papist or reputed Papist or any other in trust for any such person. Nor have we any school as yet founded or endowed within our parish. Francis Hill, vicar.

141. SPONDON

16 Nov. 1705: There is neither Papist nor reputed Papist within our parish of Spondon . . . but only one, Francis Jackson, a reputed Papist, a poor man and stockinger by trade. Samuel Fletcher, vicar; William Walker and John Cavingham, churchwardens.

142. SPONDON WITH THE CHAPELS OF CHADDESDEN AND STANLEY

1706: This may certify whom it may concern that there is neither Papist nor reputed Papist in the parish of Spondon in the county of Derby saving Francis Jackson, a frameworker, and Robert Needham of the same trade, both persons of mean condition, and that the presentation of our church is not in the hands of any Papist or reputed Papist or in the hands of any person in trust for any Papist; neither is our school in the gift or nomination of any Papist or reputed Papist. Samuel Fletcher, vicar.

143. STANLEY*

1705: Pursuant to an order of the Lords Spiritual and Temporal I do certify that there are Richard Needham, a Papist, who formerly practiced physick and Robert Needham, his son, a Papist, a stockinger by trade, which is all the Papists or reputed Papists in the chapelry of Stanley. Samuel Fletcher, vicar.
1706: see 142.

144. STANTON BY THE BRIDGE

28 June 1705: Nil Return. A. Hammond, rector; Henry Bostock and Philip Degge, churchwardens.

4 Oct. 1706: These are to certify whom it may concern that there are no Papists nor reputed Papists dwelling in the parish of Stanton juxta Pontem in the county of Derby, and that the advowson of the rectory of the aforesaid place is not in the hands of any such persons aforesaid or any other in trust for any such person, and there are no schools in the foresaid town of Stanton. Alan Hammond, rector.

145. STANTON BY DALE

1705: Nil Return. John Houlmes, Samuel Wrigley, churchwardens.

146. STANTON BY DALE AND ILKESTON

3 Oct. 1706: These are to certify whom it may concern that as to the respective persons, qualities and estates of the Papists or reputed Papists in the parishes of Stanton juxta Dale and of Ilkeston in the county of Derby, an exact and particular account of which is required to be given in at the probate court held at Derby October 4 this present year 1706. That in the parishes aforesaid there is but an inconsiderable number of them, and they of a mean quality: in the parish of Stanton juxta Dale none; in the parish of Ilkeston, two diligent stocking weavers poor, one day labourer and an exciseman's wife—the day labourer a married man, having a family and children, but himself a traveller about the country—not being of an unquiet or uncivil disposition or carriage any of them. The two stocking weavers and the exciseman's wife sojourners lately come into the parish of Ilkeston. There being no Papist or reputed Papist of any quality or having the advowson or right of presentation or donation of either of my churches or of any school, nor any other in trust for any such person. We have also in the parish of Ilkeston aforesaid one reputed Papist, a widow which has about £3 per annum in land, very poor and in debt: her name, Mrs. Mary Brooks, a stocking weaver's widow, herself, if I mistake not, of a good family of the Babingtons, that very rarely comes to church and goes not to no Divine Service. She is reported to be of a popish family. The exciseman's wife is Mrs. Witcherley ,the stocking weavers' names William Jackson and one Blouth, alias Hanforth, the day labourer's name John Holland. Humphrey Courtman, minister.

147. STAPENHILL

28 June 1705: Nil Return. Abraham Swaine, vicar; John Orme and John Godfrey, churchwardens.

148. STAPENHILL AND CALDWELL

29 July 1706: I, Abraham Swaine, vicar of Staplehill and Caldwell in the county and archdeaconry of Derby, do hereby certify that there is no Papist nor reputed Papist within this parish, that there is no school in tha same, and that the right of presentation to our church doth not belong to any Papist or reputed Papist.

149. STAVELEY

1705: The Papists or reputed Papists in the parish of Staveley . . . are as followeth: Henry Norman and his wife, farmer; Anne Steele, widow, farmer:

Gervase Gee, labourer, John Gee and his wife, William Gee and his wife, George Gee, paupers. Ralph Heathcote, rector.

1 Sept. 1706: An exact and particular account of all the Papists in the parish of Staveley in the county of Derby: Henry Norman of Inkersall, a cottager of 40s per annum or thereabouts and his wife; John Gee, a poor collier, and his wife, William Gee, a poor collier, and his wife, Matthew Gee, a poor blind man, all of Moorside; Anne Loe, a poor woman of Woodthorpe. The right of donation or presentation of the church and free school is not in the disposition of any Papist or reputed Papist or any other in trust for such persons. Ralph Heathcote, rector.

150. STONEY MIDDLETON

14 Nov. 1705: Nil Return. John Walker, curate.

2 Oct. 1706: These are to certify whom it may concern that there's no Papists nor reputed Papists within the chapelry of Stoney Middleton, that there's no school founded within the said liberty and that the presentation of the chapel of Middleton is in the hands of no Papist nor reputed Papist. John Walker, curate; James Finey and William Bower, chapelwardens.

151. STRETTON EN LE FIELD

5 Oct. 1705: Nil Return. George Gretton, rector.

4 Oct. 1706: This is to certify that there are no Papists nor reputed Papists dwelling within the parish of Stretton le Field . . . I do hereby humbly inform your lordship that the advowson or right of presentation of the church of Stretton le Field . . . is not in the disposition of any Papist or reputed Papist or any other in trust for any such person. There is no school in the above parish of Stretton le Field. George Gretton, rector.

152. SUDBURY

17 Nov. 1705: Nil Return. Samuel Sturges, rector.

3 Oct. 1706: Nil Return. Samuel Sturges, rector.

153. SUTTON CUM DUCKMANTON*

1705: This is to certify that in the parish of Sutton cum Duckmanton of what Papists we have in our parish are as follows: Richard Pickering, Mary Pickering, Thomas Cuzen, Catherine Carter senior, Catherine Carter junior. This Richard Pickering rents a farm but hath no land of his own. The rest are poor people. R. Heathcote, rector; William Marsh and George Clark, churchwardens.

1706: A particular and exact account of all the Papists or reputed Papists in the parish of Sutton cum Duckmanton in the county of Derby: Richard Pickering, farmer; Mary Pickering, his sister, Thomas Cosen, their nephew, Catherine Carter, widow, Catherine Carter, her daughter, all very poor; ——— Beveridge, a reputed Papist living in London hath an estate in Sutton valued at £28 per annum. The advowson of the living and disposition of a bible school doth not belong to any Papist or reputed Papist. Ralph Heathcote, rector.

154. SUTTON ON THE HILL

28 June 1705: There are no Papists or reputed Papists except Piercy Fairbrother, widow and tenant to a farm of about £16 per annum, aged sixty years and upwards, and Martha, her daughter, aged forty years and upwards. John Tatam.

3 Oct. 1706: Piercy Fairbrother, a poor widow aged above threescore and ten, is the only Papist or reputed Papist in the parish, and no Papist or reputed Papist hath anything to do with our church or with any school in this parish. John Tatam, vicar.

155. SWARKESTON

28 June 1705: Nil Return. Richard Fisher, William Fairfield, churchwardens.

4 Oct. 1706: These are to certify whom it may concern that there is only one Papist dwelling in the parish of Swarkeston in the county of Derby, by name William Thompson, footboy or servant to the Countess of Bellamont, and that the advowson of the rectory or the foresaid Swarkeston is not in the hands of any Papist or reputed Papist or any in trust for any such person, and there is no school in the foresaid place. Thomas Jackson, rector.

156. TADDINGTON

17 Nov. 1705: This is to certify whom it may concern that we have but one reputed Papist within our liberty of Taddington in the county of Derby: William Hodkinson, a reputed Papist, pauper. William Ratcliffe, curate.

7 Oct. 1706: Nil Return. William Ratcliffe, curate.

157. THORPE

28 June 1705: Nil Return. Alexander Hamilton, rector; John Hatfield and Ralph Clarke, churchwardens.

10 Oct. 1706: Nil Return. Alexander Hamilton, rector.

158. TIBSHELF

8 Nov. 1705: Nil Return. William Walker, vicar.

30 Sept. 1706: Nil Return. William Walker, vicar.

159. TICKNALL AND CALKE

14 Nov. 1705: Nil Return. Thomas Bate, curate.

160. TICKNALL

12 Oct. 1706: These are to certify that there is no Papist or reputed Papist in the parish of Ticknall in the archdeaconry of Derby; neither is the right of the donation of the church in the disposition of any Papist or reputed Papist. There is no school founded in the parish. Thomas Bate, curate.

161. TIDESWELL*

17 Nov. 1705: A list of the Papist and reputed Papists in the towns of Tideswell, Litton and Wheston . . . are as followeth viz: John Alleyn, gentleman, £40 per annum; John Hardy, yeoman, £4 per annum; Henry Bocking, farmer; Richard Palfreyman, miller; Thomas Berchinhough, pauper; George Chapman, pauper; William Bates, pauper; Francis Varnon, pauper; Katherine Hauge, sempster; Emmot Palphreman, spinster; Thomas Bocking, pauper; John Wild, pauper; John Berchinough, pauper; Robert Needham, pauper. John Allen, vicar.

31 Jan. 1707: The Papists or reputed Papists within the parish of Tideswell in the county of Derby are as followeth: **Tideswell:** John Allen, gentleman, £40 per annum; John Hardy, yeoman, £3 per annum; Henry Bocking, farmer; Joan Crooks, spinster; Thomas Bagshaw, grocer; Richard Palfreyman, miller; Katherine Hague, spinster; Emmot Palfreyman, spinster; William Bates, pauper; Francis Vernon, pauper; Elizabeth Oldfield, pauper; Thomas Berchinhough, pauper. **Wheston:** Mrs. Agnes Freeman, spinster; Mrs. Anne Allen, spinster; John Birchinhough, servant; John Wild, servant; Robert Needham, pauper. **Litton:** Elizabeth Bocking. **Wormhill:** George Thornehill, yeoman, £5 per annum; Wilfrid Gill, farmer; Stephen Gill, farmer; Helen Bramwall, spinster; George Bowden, blacksmith; Gervase Smith,

carpenter; Gervase Torr, yeoman, £9 per annum; John Torr, farmer; Elizabeth Hambleton, spinster. I, John Allen vicar of Tideswell, do certify that none of these persons have any presentation to any living or nomination to any school. John Allen.

162. TISSINGTON

28 June 1705: Nil Return. Luke Flint, curate; Thomas Redferne and John Johnson, churchwardens.

4 Oct. 1706: Nil Return. Luke Flint, curate.

163. TRUSLEY

15 Nov. 1705: Nil Return. Robert Solden, rector.

4 Oct. 1706: These are humbly to certify that we have neither Papist nor reputed Papist in our town or parish. Neither does the presentation to our rectory of Trusley belong to either Papist or reputed Papist nor any person in trust for them. We have no school in our parish. Robert Solden, rector.

164. TURNDITCH

28 June 1705: Nil Return. John Nuton (?); Robert Tanner.

1706: No Return.

165. TWYFORD

28 June 1705: Nil Return: Samuel Holmes, Richard Ensor, chaplewardens.

1706: No Return.

166. WALTON UPON TRENT

28 June 1705: Nil Return. Thomas Taylor, Francis Hall, churchwardens.

1706: We do hereby certify your lordship that we have no Papists or reputed Papists dwelling in our parish; neither is the right of presentation or donation of our church in the disposition of any Papist or reputed Papist, nor have we any school at all founded within our parish. William Tunnicliffe, William Reanalls, churchwardens.

167. WEST HALLAM*

28 June 1705: An exact accompt of all Papists in the parish of West Hallam in the county of Derby exhibted at a court held at Derby: George Pegg, farmer, his rent is about £40 per annum; John Werden, farmer of £12 per annum; Hugh Jackson, labourer, he rents lands at £4 16s per annum; John Dakin, stocking-maker; Peter Bennet, labourer; Thomas Cater, bagpiper; William Cater, pauper.

I cannot learn what any of these persons are worth, but it is verily thought that, if their debts were paid, the remainder of all their estates would amount to very little. Henry Greatorex, rector.

4 Oct. 1706: A true list of all the Papists or reputed Papists in the parish of West Hallam . . . together with an exact account of their quality, estates and place of abode delivered at the probate court held at Derby by the Right Worshipful William Walmesley, chancellor of the diocese of Lichfield and Coventry aforesaid or his deputy on the 4th day of October Anno Domini 1706: George Pegg, farmer, who holds about £40 per annum; John Werden, farmer of about £12 per annum; Hugh Jackson, cottager, who leaseth about £6 per annum; John Dakin and two sons near Man's estate that live with him, all framework-knitters; Widow Mosse and one son with her, framework-knitters; Peter Bennet, labourer; Thomas Cater, piper; William Cater, pauper. These all live in the parish of West Hallam aforesaid

and are so low in the world that it is questioned whether (after their debts are paid) the estates of all together will amount to £30. Neither our church nor school is in the donation of any Papist or reputed Papist nor of any other intrusted for them that I know of or believe. H. Greatorex, rector.

168. WESTON UPON TRENT

28 June 1705: Nil Return. Thomas Gilbert, George Dornelaw, churchwardens.

3 Oct. 1706: These are to certify to your lordship that there is but one popish family in the parish of Weston upon Trent in the county of Derby. The man's name is Brown, a farmer. His family consists beside himself of a wife, his mother and sister and six children. We have no endowed school; neither does the advowson of the church belong to any Papist or reputed Papist or of any in trust for such persons. E. Holden, rector.

169. WHITTINGTON

26 June 1705: Nil Return. Thomas Collice, rector; George Gilberthorpe and James Nalor, churchwardens.

1 Oct. 1706: These are to certify that there are no Papists or reputed Papists dwelling within the parish of Whittngton in the county of Derby (except one Edward Nettleton who is sometimes a journeyman to an hatter in the foresaid parish), and that the right of presentation or donation of the church or school in that town is in the disposition of any Papist or reputed Papist or any in trust for them. Thomas Callice, rector.

170. WHITWELL

25 June 1705: Frances Parker, widow, Papist, a poor old woman. Lewis Griffins, rector.

2 Oct. 1706: These are to certify that we have no Papists or reputed Papists in our parish aforesaid but Frances Parker, a very poor widow. No Papist or so reputed in our parish has any presentation to any living or nomination to any school. Lewis Griffin, rector.

171. WILLESLEY

14 Nov. 1705: Nil Return. John Chawner, headbury.

1 Oct. 1706: These are humbly to certify that in the parish of Willesley in the county of Derby there is no Papist nor reputed Papist nor any school or school lands in the parish nor is the advowson or right of presentation to that living in the hand of any Papist or reputed Papist or any other in trust for any such person. W. Lynes, curate.

172. WILLINGTON

28 June 1705: Nil Return. John Choice, curate; Joseph Downes and Simon Ball, churchwardens.

1706: These are to certify that upon the best information I can have there are no Papists nor reputed Papists residing within the liberties of Willington in the county of Derby, nor doth the advowson of the church or right of presentation belong to any Papist or reputed Papist or any other in trust for any such person. There is no school in the parish. John Choice, minister.

173. WINGERWORTH*

26 June 1705: The certificate of the minister and churchwardens of Wingerworth . . . is as follows: There is dwelling within the parish of Wingerworth Sir Henry

Hunlock, a Papist, who hath about £1000 per annum, and he hath Francis Hardwick, Sybil Prichett, servants, that are Papists. There is Thomas Lee, and Jane, his wife, Papists, within the parish, Samuel Greensmith and Anne, his wife, Alice Tholmiston, all Papists, and none others. Matthew Furnis, curate; Edward Davenport and Henry Stringfellow, churchwardens.

2 Oct. 1706: These are further to satisfy that within our parish of Wingerworth there are these following Papists and reputed Papists whose names are as follows, viz: Henry Hunloke, knight and baronet, and all his family, estate £1,000 per annum; Samuel Greensmith, his wife and one child, husbandman, rent £20 per annum; Thomas Lee and his wife and three children, husbandman, £7 per annum; Alice Tomlinson; Widow Brown, reputed one, a farmer, rent £10 per annum; Mary Davenport and her two children; Elizabeth Barber. Our church is impropriate and the Reverend the Dean of Lincoln is both the parson and impropriator. As for our school we have not any that is in the disposition of any Papist or reputed Papist or any other in trust for any such person or persons. Matthew Furnis, curate; John Child and Lawrence Easthwate, churchwardens.

174. WINSTER

28 June 1705: Nil Return. Joseph Hayne, curate; Christopher Bagshaw and Robert Toples, churchwardens.

5 Oct. 1706: Nil Return. William Newton; Daniel Jagman and Edward Bunting, chapelwardens.

175. WIRKSWORTH

29 June 1705: Nil Return. Robert Toplis, John Shaw, churchwardens.

1706: No Return.

176. WORMHILL

1705: The Papists or reputed Papists in the chapelry of Wormhill . . . are as followeth: George Thornhill, yeoman, about £5 or £6 per annum; Wilfrid Gill, farmer; Stephen Gill, farmer; Helen Bramwall, spinster; George Bowden, blacksmith; Gervase Smith, carpenter; Gervase Torr, yeoman, about £9 or £10 per annum; John Torr, farmer; Elizabeth Hambleton, spinster. Roger Wilkson, curate.

1706: See 161.

177. YOULGREAVE

26 June 1705: Nil Return. Edward Moore, vicar; Latham Clark, William Millard and Francis Ashburne, churchwardens.

14 April 1707: Nil Return.

Notes to the Returns

4. ASHBOURNE

The Whitehalls of Yeldersley had a long history of Catholicism. In 1595 it was reported: At Mr. Whitehall's house near Ashbourne, four miles from "Awkmonton" (Alkmanton), lieth one Robert Shewall, a seminary priest, with a bald head, having one leg bigger than the other, and at the buttery door they go up a pair of stairs straight to achamber where they say mass, and Tanfield (another seminary priest) useth thither often'.[1] However, the Whitehall's tradition of Catholicism was not unbroken. There is no record of any member of this family suffering for faith in Derbyshire between the conviction of Ellen Whitehall for recusancy in 1607 and the payment of double subsidy in 1641 by Anne Whitehall as a popish recusant.[2] Evidence of catholic recusancy in the parish of Ashbourne is also lacking during the same period. The revival of Catholicism in the Whitehall family may have stemmed from a marriage alliance with the Pegges. Anne Whitehall was the daughter of Christopher Pegge of Yeldersley, whose widow, Jane, was also financially mulcted as a recusant in 1641.[3] Jane was the daughter of Rowland Eyre of Hassop, progenitor of the Catholic Eyres of Hassop. Whatever was the case a group of Catholics from the mid seventeenth century clustered around the Pegges and Whitehalls in Yeldersley and Ashbourne. Ten Papists were reported in the Compton Census of 1676. The following draft letter to Bishop Stonor, vicar-apostolic of the Midland District, dated 12 March 1740, reveals that a mission with a priest was established at Yeldersley largely through the efforts of the Whitehalls: 'By different contributions of three or four of the family of Whitehalls . . . amongst whom was a good priest, so much money was formerly raised as was sufficient to create a rent of £13 per annum for the assistant of the parish thereabouts, which parish as late Mr. Stanford (the Catholic priest of Wingerworth) . . . has oftentimes declared was always looked upon equally to comprehend Roston and Norbury and parts adjacent as well as the township itself of Yeldersley. The money so raised came into the hands of Mr. Gilbert Whitehall, who became head of the family, and being suitor to Mrs. Margaret Brent . . . and dying during his courtship, made the said Mrs. Margaret his executrix and heiress of his estate, desiring moreover upon his deathbed that she would add £7 per annum more to the foundation of Yeldersley . . .' [4]

1. PRO, State Papers Domestic, SP12/251/14.
2. PRO, Recusant Roll E377/15; Subsidy Roll 1641 E179/94/371.
3. J. Hunter, **Familia Minorum Gentiae** (Harleian Society, xxvii-xxix, 1894-6), 305.
4. AAB, Draft Letter A79.

9. BAKEWELL

The vicar of Bakewell's off-hand tone in his returns gives a misleading impression. The Eyres of Hassop were one of the wealthiest Derbyshire Catholic families with extensive estates in the Peak and elsewhere. In 1717, when Papists were required by Act of Parliament to register their estates at the Quarter Sessions, Rowland Eyre of Hassop enjoyed an annual gross income of £1,115 and his eldest son Thomas £561. Two other members of the family possessed life interests in part of the estates amounting to £250 per annum.[1] The Eyres had been openly Catholic since the days of Rowland's grandfather and had formed a substantial Catholic community around them at Hassop. Sixty-five Papists were returned in the

Compton Census of 1676 and forty, including a 'reputed priest', in the Papist Returns of 1767.[2] It is unfortunate the vicar of Bakewell made little effort to list the community in 1705-6.

1. PRO, Forfeited Estates Papers FEC1/1139.
2. HLRO, Papist Returns, abstract, 1767.

10. BARLBOROUGH

Catholicism in Barlborough stemmed from two sources. The Poles of Spinkhill (see Eckington), living near the parish boundary, were an undoubted influence. A younger branch of this family purchased Park Hall and established a Jesuit mission there.[1] However, German Pole of Park Hall (died 1687) was the last Catholic of his line. His son and heir was brought up as a conformist. The other Catholic influence in Barlborough stemmed from the minor gentry families who owned Beighton Fields Priory. During the earlier half of the seventeenth century the property was held by the Hewitts who were succeeded by the Bowdens.[2] In 1717 Henry Bowden registered his estate at an annual value of £36 11s. 7d.[3]

1. R. Meredith, 'The Eyres of Hassop and their Forfeited Estates', **Recusant History**, viii (1965), 62; H. Foley, **The Records of the English Province of the Society of Jesus** (London, 1881) v, 478.
2. Hunter, op.cit., 358.
3. PRO, Forfeited Estates Papers FEC1/1139.

12. BARROW-UPON-TRENT

The first references to Catholicism in the Beaumont family are the convictions of John Beaumont and his wife in 1658 for Catholic Recusancy.[1] His faith may have stemmed from his first marriage to Dorothy daughter of John Powtrell of West Hallam (see under West Hallam). His son, Robert, was disarmed as a Papist in 1690 and registered his Derbyshire estates in 1717 at £86 14s per annum.[2] Although Robert Norman denied that any Papist held the presentation to the living, the advowson was in fact owned by the Beaumonts. Indeed Norman admitted as much in a contemporary letter he wrote about the endowments of his church. The Beaumonts had not presented to the living since 1638. Afterwards they had allowed conformists the privilege. Robert Norman had been presented to his vicarage by Nicholas Wilmot in 1675.[3]

1. PRO, Recusant Roll E377/63.
2. DRO, Quarter Sessions Order Book i, 179; PRO, Forfeited Estates Papers FEC1/1139.
3. Derby Reference Library, Church Notes c. 1705. MS.9550; LJRO Liber Cleri 1639, B/V/1/62; PRO, Bishop's Certificate to the First Fruits and Tenths Office E331/Coventry and Lichfield/21

13. BARTON BLOUNT

Stress was laid on Merry Simpson's conformity in the 1705 returns because his religious loyalties and inclinations were uncertain, and appear to have been in a state of flux. His mother was the daughter and heiress of Henry Merry of Barton Blount, whose family had a history of staunch Catholicism since Elizabeth's reign. In 1595 it was reported: 'Item, at Mr. Merry's house in Barton Park . . . lieth one Nicholas Wade alias Yeke, a seminary priest, and he is often at Mr. Palmer's of Kegworth'.[1] Despite this Catholic background Simpson had been educated at Protestant establishments at Repton and Cambridge, although he had not taken a degree at Cambridge, probably to avoid the religious tests involved.[2] Difficulties arose over Simpson's right of presentation to the rectory of Barton Blount. By Acts of Parliament of 1603-4 and 1689 ecclesiastical patronage belonging to popish recusants convict or to Papists refusing the oath of allegiance of 1689 was to devolve upon the two universities. Simpson was allowed to present to the living in 1689 only after he had secured a certificate from the clerk of the peace that he had not been presented nor convicted as a Papist. He presented John Alsop in 1696, but only on the bishop's condition that Alsop upon bond of £200 agreed to resign if Simpson's right to present in that turn was discovered to have been void.[3] Simpson was presented at the Quarter Sessions as a Papist, together with his mother, twice in 1693 and twice in 1695. Thereafter only his mother (in 1698 and 1699) was presented.[4] As a demonstration of his conformity it was probably he who repaired and restored the church at Barton Blount for use. However, in 1717 he registered his estates as a Papist at an annual gross value of £346 17s. His estates were heavily mortgaged and, as a result, his nephew and successor sold them in the 1730s and retired to a French monastery.[5]

1. PRO, State Papers Domestic SP12/251/14.
2. Venn, **Alumni Cantabrigienses.**
3. LJRO, Presentation Deeds B/A/3, Barton Blount.
4. DRO, Quarter Sessions Papers 1693, 1695, 1698, 1699.
5. PRO, Forfeited Estates Papers FEC1/1139.

37. CHAPEL EN LE FRITH

Henry Kirke registered his estate under the Papists' Estates Registration Act. His annual rental was then £18 15s besides the income from his estates he farmed himself.[1]

1. PRO, Forfeited Estates Papers FEC1/1139.

49. DALE ABBEY

Robert Needham was the son of Richard Needham of Stanley Grange. Both were mentioned in Stephen Dugdale's deposition of 17 January 1679 because Dugdale claimed Richard Needham had acted as a messenger of the Jesuits involved in the Popish Plot (for Richard Needham see under Stanley). According to Dugdale Robert knew nothing of the plot for his father had told him: 'For although his son was a good Christian enough, yet that (the Popish Plot) was not a thing to be trusted to everyone'.[1] In 1690 the Quarter Sessions banned Robert Needham and Joseph Baker from keeping alehouses in Dale Abbey for allowing 'evil rule and disorder to be kept in their houses' and for entertaining 'persons that speak in derogation of the government.[2] As a Catholic Needham had no liking for the Revolution of 1688.

1. HMC, Fitzherbert MSS, 13th report part vi, 125.
2. DRO, Quarter Sessions Order Book i, 179.

59. DRONFIELD

The main Papist family in the parish were the Eyres. The family had been Catholic from the sixteenth century when their seat had been Holme Hall, Newbold, in Chesterfield parish. Edward Eyre married a sister of Robert Pursglove, suffragan bishop of Hull, who was deprived in 1559 for refusing to take the oath of Supremacy. His son married a daughter of John Fitzherbert, imprisoned for harbouring Catholic priests (see Hathersage). One of this family had sheltered St. Edmund Campion in 1581.[1] During the early eighteenth century Vincent Eyre acted as an agent for the Jesuits of the Derbyshire District.[2] When he registered his estates he valued his Dronfield estates at £63 17s 6d per annum and his total estate at £112 15s 6d.[3]

1. G. Anstruther, **Vaux of Harrowden** (Newport, 1953), 137.
2. Mount St. Mary's College, Spinkhill, Account Book.
3. PRO, Forfeited Estates Papers FEC1/1139.

61-2. ECKINGTON

In this parish one of the largest Catholic communities of Derbyshire had grown up around the Poles of Spinkhill who had been Papists since Elizabeth's reign. John Pole, mentioned in the returns, was the last male of the line. Spinkhill had long been served by Jesuits. The Poles had strong attachments to the Society of Jesus since seven members of the Spinkhill branch of the family and two of the Park Hall branch had entered the order. The priest mentioned in the returns was Robert Percy alias Francis Smith S.J. who probably served Spinkhill from 1684 until his death in 1715.[1] This Jesuit is the only Catholic priest mentioned in the Papist Returns for Derbyshire. The following Catholics registered their estates in 1717: John Pole of Spinkhill £201 10s 10d per annum; John Marshall of Killamarsh £18 per annum; Anne Savage of Eckington £20 per annum (probably George's widow); Thomas Howson £8 per annum.[2]

1. H. Foley, **The Records of the English Province of the Society of Jesus,** vii, 587.
2. PRO, Forfeited Estates Papers, FEC1/1139.

63. EDENSOR

On 26 June 1705 the churchwardens handed in a glebe terrier to the bishop's visitation court which also contains the following presentment more detailed than the Papist Return of the same date: 'And there is no alteration in the state of our church or parish. We have no Papist or legal inhabitant of our parish; only one by virtue of a certificate (of settlement under the Act of Settlement of 1662) resides here from Tideswell, named Michael Sherwood, and gets his living by day labour'.[1]

1. DRO, Glebe Terriers 57 Edensor.

76. GLOSSOP

Although large estates and the advowson of the church belonged to the Howards (Earls of Arundel and Dukes of Norfolk) the history of the family's Catholicism during the seventeenth century had been so erratic that they had had little or no influence on the religion of the inhabitants of Glossop. However, during the eighteenth century there was a change. By 1767 there were nineteen Papists in Glossop including a 'reputed priest'.[1] By the Acts of 1605-6 and 1689 Catholic recusants or trustees acting on their behalf were not allowed to present clergymen to benefices, and their rights were supposed to devolve upon the two universities (Cambridge in the case of Derbyshire). Had it been certain that George Howard was a Catholic recusant neither he nor his trustees could have made a presentation to the vicarage. However, their right to present William Bagshaw was not questioned by the bishop in 1703.[2]

1. HLRO, Papist Returns 1767, abstract.
2. LJRO, Bishop Hough's Register B/A/1/19.

78. HATHERSAGE

It is not clear from this return that the parish of Hathersage had probably more Catholics than any other parish in Derbyshire. The Catholic community was also one of the oldest in Derbyshire. Its origins can be traced back to the influence of the Fitzherberts, lords of the manors of Padley and Hathersage, during Elizabeth's reign. In 1577 Bishop Bentham of Coventry and Lichfield named John Fitzherbert and his wife of Hathersage among those prominent in Derbyshire for their refusal to attend Anglican services.[1] The same John was arrested for harbouring Nicholas Garlick and Robert Ludlam, two seminary priests, at Padley manor house in July 1588. He was imprisoned for the rest of his life and the two priests were martyred at Derby. Although the Fitzherbert estates were seized and eventually sold[2] Catholicism survived in the parish among the yeomen and husbandmen. On account of its remoteness the Catholic community in Hathersage was one of the very few Catholic communities in Derbyshire which did not depend for survival upon the Catholic gentry. Hence in the episcopal returns of conventicles of 1669 the Hathersage Catholics were noted as 'people of mean quality'.[3] Large numbers of Catholics from Hathersage were brought to the attention of the authorities during the seventeenth century. In March 1616, 77 parishioners were convicted for recusancy and in 1639 73.[4] The Compton Census returns reported 140 Papists in Hathersage in 1676 while in in the same year 117 popish recusants were cited after an episcopal visitation.[5] At the Michaelmas Quarter Sessions of 1693 63 popish recusants were presented.[6] Although these figures include Catholic wives, widows and adolescents, and the Papist Return of 1705 does not, they indicate that the vicar of Hathersage probably underestimated the strength of Catholicism in his parish in 1705. The plebian Catholicism of Hathersage and its lack of gentry backing is indicated by the number of freeholders registering small estates there in 1717. They were: Dorothy Smilter, rent not set forth as the estate was in her own occupation; George Green, rent not set forth as the estate was in his own occupation; Thomas Furnis, rent not set forth as the estate was in his own occupation; Thomas Eyre, one messuage in his own occupation and an annual rent of 9s; Thomas Eyre, rents of £21 per annum; John Smilter, rents not set forth as the estate was in his own and Dorothy Smilter's occupation; Anne Haigh of Penistone, Yorkshire, annual rent of £16.[7] The return makes no mention of a priest. George Bostock alias West is first mentioned as serving the mission in the High Peak of Derbyshire in c.1692 and ministered there continuously until his death at Hathersage in December 1727.[8]

1. PRO, State Papers Domestic SP12/118/17, 28.1.
2. R .Meredith, 'The Sale of the Hathersage Estates in the 1650s', **DAJ**, xc (1970), 32-55.
3. G. L. Turner, **Original Records of Early Nonconformity under Persecution and Indulgence** (London, 1911) i, 54.
4. PRO, Recusant Rolls E377/22, 46.
5. LJRO, Citations B/V/4, 1677 (Archdeaconry of Derby).
6. DRO, Quarter Sessions Papers 1693.
7. PRO, Forfeited Estates Papers FEC1/1139.
8. G. Anstruther, **The Seminary Priests** (Great Wakering, 1976), iii, 21.

81. HEANOR

The Lowe family only appear in records as Catholics during the second half of the seventeenth century. Their Catholicism seems to have stemmed from their family connections with the Eyres of Dronfield (see Dronfield). Charles Lowe's mother first married Thomas Eyre of Dronfield and was thus grandmother of the Vincent Eyre named in the Papist Returns The Lowes failed to establish a Catholic community around them in Heanor parish because when Charles died in 1709 he divided most of his estates between his three daughters. The small residue he bequeathed to his brother Anthony.

92. KNIVETON

The family which 'perverted' Tipper were presumably the Merrys of Kniveton, a younger branch of the Merrys of Barton Blount. Gilbert Merry registered his Kniveton estates in 1717 at £60 13s per annum.[1] It is possible that the Merrys had temporarily left the parish because registrations of the births of Gilbert's children appear in Kniveton parish registers in 1702, 1703, 1707 and 1708. There are also no records of the baptisms of William Tipper's children in the same register; only the registration of the birth of his son Thomas appears in it on 4 December 1704.[2]

1. PRO, Forfeited Estates Papers FEC1/1139.
2. DRO, Kniveton Parish Register Transcript 1649-1791 D.1139.

112. NORBURY

There was resistance in Norbury against the Church Settlement of 1559 from the beginning. Henry Cumberford ,the rector, was deprived of his benefice for refusing the Oath of Supremacy in 1559. By 1561 Sir Thomas Fitzherbert, the lord of the manor, was in the Fleet Prison for his religious views. Except for short periods he spent the rest of his life in prison until his death in the Tower in 1591. Under the Fitzherberts' influence many others in the parish rejected the reformed Established Church. In 1577 the bishop of Coventry and Lichfield reported sixteen inhabitants as notorious for their refusal to go to church.[1] In the Epiphany Quarter Sessions of 1626 35 parishioners were convicted as popish recusants.[2] 74 conformists and 65 Papists were returned in the Compton Census, the highest concentration of Papists reported in any Derbyshire parish. On the death of Sir John Fitzherbert of Norbury in 1649 his estates passed to the Swynnerton branch of the Fitzherberts. As they possessed large estates in Staffordshire and Shropshire they were usually absentee landlords. Not one member of the family appears in the Constables' Presentments in the Quarter Sessions Papers between 1693 and 1732. It is clear from the returns that William Fitzherbert employed an agent to look after his Norbury estates. Under the Catholic Adams this arrangement does not appear to have affected Catholicism in Norbury, but in 1726 John Stanford, the priest at Wingerworth wrote: 'It grieves me much to see how religion is likely to decay in that country. Mr. Stones, Mr. Fitzherbert's steward, hath put in so bad a man to Norbury Hall that I do not see how the poor Catholics can be saved there'.[3] Although the returns make no mention of it a Catholic mission was well-established in Norbury and was served by secular priests who also served the mission at Yeldersley (see Ashbourne). Registration records make it clear that Catholicism remained strong and that the rector felt keenly the presence of a Catholic mission in his parish. On the front page of the parish register are notes of a number of Catholic burials, for example: "Memorandum: Jane Palmer (being eighty years old or thereabouts and turned a Papist) was laid in Norbury churchyard . . . 1719 without any funeral office, and . . . Mr. Harding took sixpence for an affidavit; Memorandum: Mr. William Adams (dying under the sentence of excommunication as by an order of the chancellor's court procured by my curate Mr. Harding and Mr. Bill) was laid in Norbury church without any funeral office 1st September 1720".[4] In the bishop's transcripts of the registers is the following note: "Born Lettice, the daughter of Mr. William and Mrs. Anne Adams, 8th November christened by a popish priest".[5] In 1717 the following Catholics registered their estates with valuations: William Fitzherbert, esquire, £497 15s per annum; John Goodman of Madeley, Shropshire, gentleman, £5 per annum; Constance Halford £10 per annum; John Bill £7 per annum; William Adams of Marston Montgomery £52 14s 6d per annum; John Mold, rent not set forth; John Oldacre, rent not set forth; Mr. Thomas Dakin in Roston £15 per annum.[6]

1. PRO, State Papers Domestic SP12/18/17.
2. PRO, Recusant Roll E377/31.
3. AAB, Letter from J. Stanford to E. Dicconson 1726, A 674.
4. DRO, Norbury Parish Register D641/PI1.
5. LJRO, Bishop's Transcripts B/V/7 Norbury.
6. PRO, Forfeited Estates Papers FEC1/1139.

127-8. REPTON

The governors were descendants of the daughters and co-heiresses of Sir John Porte of Etwall, founder of the school. One daughter had married Sir William Gerard of Bryn, Lancashire, and their descendants retained their Catholicism.

143. STANLEY

For Robert Needham see Dale Abbey.

Dr. Richard Needham of Stanley Grange (actually within the parish of Dale Abbey) had been one of the minor informers during the Popish Plot. Stephen Dugdale, the Staffordshire informer, had claimed Needham had acted as the messenger of those Jesuits involved in plotting the assasination of Charles II and the consequent Catholic uprising in his dipostion to the Council of 17 January 1679.[1] Soon afterwards Needham had been arrested and brought before the Council. At first he denied all knowledge of a Catholic plot, but, under pressure, he had given a series of depositions mainly referring to meetings of Jesuits at West Hallam and to conversations with George Busby S.J., the chaplain of West Hallam Hall, about the general designs of the plot. In his information he merely intruded the Catholics he knew into the Plot whch had already been outlined by Dugdale and Titus Oates.[2] His burial at West Hallam is recorded on 2 June 1706.[3]

1. HMC, Fitzherbert MSS, 13th Report part vi, 125.
2. Bod. Lib., Rawlinson MSS A 135, 484-89; A 136, 84-5, 172-74, 470, 475, 486.
3. DRO, West Hallam Parish Register, D1224/PI2.

153. SUTTON CUM DUCKMANTON

The Beveridges of Sutton cum Duckmanton had been Catholics since the late sixteenth century. A John Beveridge had entered the Venerable English College, Rome, in 1593 but died there the following year; a Thomas Beveridge entered the same in 1600 and eventually joined the Society of Jesus.[1] In 1717 the following Catholics registered estates in the parish: George Beveridge £28 per annum; Mrs. Carter, rent not set forth.[2]

1. W. Kelly, **Liber Ruber Venerabilis Collegii Anglorum de Urbe** (Catholic Record Society), xxxvii, 279, 362; xl, 795.
2. PRO, Forfeited Estates Papers FEC1/1139.

161. TIDESWELL

The origins of Popish Recusancy in Tideswell went back deep into Elizabeth's reign. Although Bishop Pursglove, after losing his ecclesiastical preferments in 1559, went to some Anglican services, he proved a conservative influence in the parish during his residence there. He founded the grammar school at Tideswell and its first master, Nicholas Garlick, afterwards left to train for the priesthood at Douai. After his ordination he worked mainly in the Derbyshire Peak until he was captured at Padley Hall and executed at Derby in 1588.[1] Four of Garlick's pupils became Catholic priests. Another Catholic influence was William Fieldsend, vicar of Tideswell, who left his living in the 1570s unable to accept the reformed doctrines of the Established Church. Afterwards he wandered about the Peak as a massing priest. Tideswell was similar to Hathersage, but unlike most other Derbyshire Catholic centres, in that there was no dominant Catholic gentry family in the parish. In 1717 the following Catholics registered estates in Tideswell: Henry Bockin, lands in his own occupation; Richard Hardy, most of his lands in his own occupation; Robert Freeman £3 16s per annum; Garvase Bagshawe £8 5s per annum; George Thornhill, rent not set forth; Gervase Torr, rent not set forth; John Allen £91 1s 4d per annum; Mr. Roland Middleton of Ellerton, Staffordshire £28 15s per annum; Mrs. Helem Bromsall £2 per annum.[2]

1. E. King S.J., **Nicholas Garlick, Martyr** (London, 1904).
2. PRO, Forfeited Estates Papers FEC1/1139.

167. WEST HALLAM

Catholics had concentrated in West Hallam ever since Elizabeth's reign, supported by the Powtrells, the lords of the manor. Walter Powtrell was fined 500 marks in Star Chamber for sheltering St. Edmund Campion S.J. in 1581[1] and his wife was regularly convicted for popish recusancy until her death in 1634. During the Popish Plot West Hallam Hall was searched five times before the chaplain, George Busby, was captured. At this time one of the largest Catholic communities in Derbyshire lived in West Hallam. Forty Papists were returned in the Compton Census of 1676. Although the Powtrell male line died out in 1687 the community continued to be sustained by Catholic gentry because the Hunlokes of Wingerworth (q.v.) succeeded to the Powtrell estates. Henry Greatorex misinformed the bishop about the patronage of the church even though he must have known the true situation. The advowson was owned by the lords of the manor and in 1669 Greatorex himself had been presented to the benefice by Anne Powtrell.[2] In 1706 the Hunlokes owned the advowson and continued to do so until they sold their West Hallam estates in the 1820s.

1. G. Anstruther, **Vaux of Harrowden** (Newport, 1953), 126.
2. LJRO, Bishop Hacket's Register B/A/1, 17,

173. WINGERWORTH

Sir Henry Hunloke, named in the returns, was the first head of the family who is known to have been a Catholic. However, there had been Catholic influences at work in the family in earlier generations. His grandmother had married Anthony Stanford, a younger son of a notorious Catholic family in Staffordshire, and both husband and wife were convicted for recusancy in 1641.[1] Sir Henry's aunt married Henry Powtrell of West Hallam, Anthony Stanford's nephew. A Catholic community did not develop in Wingerworth until after the head of the Hunloke family became a Catholic and their numbers grew slowly. Four Papists were returned in the Compton Census of 1676, but by 1767 there were 75 Papists, including a reputed priest.[2] The increase in numbers was probably due to the efforts of the missioner priests living at the hall. At the time of the returns the Catholic priest was John Stanford who had been at Wingerworth since c.1692 and died there in 1737.[3] The curate of Wingerworth seriously underestimated the value of the Hunloke estates, probably because he did not account for their estates outside the Wingerworth area. When the Hunlokes registered their estates in 1717, after Sir Henry's death, they returned the following annual values: Sir Windsor Hunloke (eldest son and heir) £1035 12s 9d per annum; Lady Katherine Hunloke (Sir Henry's widow) £705 10s 11d per annum; Robert Hunloke (second son) £58 17s per annum.[4]

1. PRO, Recusant Roll E377/49.
2. HLRO, Papist Returns, abstract, 1767.
3. Anstruther, **The Seminary Priests,** iii, 209-10.
4. PRO, Forfeited Estates Papers FEC1/1139.

Index

Roman numerals refer to pages of the Introduction, arabic numbers to entries in the main text, and asterisks to entries in the Notes to the Returns.